Quiet Retreat Teachings

Book II: The Magic of Empty Teachers

Diamond Mountain University Press

dmu-press.com

More by Geshe Michael Roach:

The Principal Teachings of Buddhism (author Je Tsongkapa, compiler Geshe Michael Roach)

Preparing for Tantra: The Mountain of Blessings (authors Je Tsongkapa, Geshe Michael Roach, Lobsang Tharchin)

The Diamond Cutter:
The Buddha on Managing Your Business and Your Life

The Garden: A Parable

How Yoga Works: Healing Yourself and Others with the Yoga Sutra

The Essential Yoga Sutra: Ancient Wisdom for Your Yoga

The Tibetan Book of Yoga:
Ancient Buddhist Teachings on the Philosophy and Practice of Yoga

The Eastern Path to Heaven:
A Guide to Happiness from the Teachings of Jesus in Tibet

Karmic Management:
What Goes Around Comes Around in Your Business and Your Life

Quiet Retreat Teachings

The Magic of Empty Teachers

by Geshe Michael Roach

March 8 - 11, 2001
Diamond Mountain Retreat Center

St. David, Arizona

Diamond Mountain University Press

dmu-press.com

Diamond Mountain University Press
dmu-press.com

The Magic of Empty Teachers
Quiet Retreat Teachings
Book 2

Published in the United States by Diamond Mountain University Press
Visit our website at www.dmu-press.com

ISBN-10: 0-9837478-2-2

PRINTED IN THE UNITED STATES OF AMERICA

Book Design and Cover by Katey Fetchenhier

2 0 1 1 0 7 0 0 0 1

TABLE OF CONTENTS

First Day: Thursday, March 8, 2001   1

Second Day: Friday, March 9, 2001   15

Third Day: Saturday, March 10, 2001   56

Fourth Day: Sunday, March 11, 2001   75

Verses   92

Acknowledgements   98

Preface

"And so the process
Of making your perfect Teacher
Makes you perfect;
This itself is the teaching,
The magic of empty teachers."
– Geshe Michael Roach

Between March 3, 2000 and June 6, 2003, Geshe Michael Roach and several of his senior students engaged in a three-year silent meditation retreat in the desert wilderness of southeastern Arizona. During that time he didn't see anyone apart from the six retreatants, didn't get any news from the outside world, and didn't even hear the sound of a human voice. However, in order to fulfill a promise he had made to his students before he left, Geshe Michael came blindfolded to the edge of the retreat boundary twice a year to teach, and students came from all over the world to listen to these teachings.

In the Spring of 2001, almost 200 students arrived in southeastern Arizona for the second Quiet Retreat Teachings. We filled up motel rooms in Tombstone, bunked with the retreat caretakers, and camped out under the desert sky. Some of us had been students of Geshe Michael's for years; others had never met him before the three-year retreat began. Still we cooked for each other, shared teachings, and gathered supplies from the Circle K gas station for our evening hours in the Arizona wilderness where the retreat teachings took place; after the first teachings we knew we'd need blankets for warmth once the sun went down, food to pass around on the breaks, and water to share. It felt like a joyful reunion—we were becoming family.

Each day at the appointed time we'd gather in the parking lot of a Mexican restaurant and wait for the pilot car to lead us snaking through the winding back-roads out to the teaching site, where we were met so graciously by the retreat staff.

To say it was rustic is an understatement. The retreaters lived in yak-felt yurts that had been imported from Mongolia and set on a knoll near a wash with oak trees and mesquite, at the foot of a small mountain range, about half an hour down a dirt road, on open range land, with no other buildings for miles. There was no electricity, no running water, none of the comforts of civilization. In the summers, the temperature rose to well over 100 degrees, interspersed with relentless monsoon rains; in the winters there was driving wind and snow. The caretaker's site consisted of a tiny kitchen yurt, two small caretaker yurts, and a tent where Ven. Jigme lived.

And so the lives of both retreatants and caretakers required strong dedication and purpose.

But there was also incredible beauty: blazing sunsets, brilliant lightning displays in desert storms, vivid cactus blossoms, songbirds, the huge desert sky, the brilliance of the stars and the milky way and in the quiet of their solitude. The animals of the desert came to trust them and to become their friends.

We enjoyed that beauty on our now familiar trek through the wide wash on ground that vacillated between dry, hot dust and boot-grabbing mud. The teachings were held where the wash flattened out, at the edge of the retreat boundary. The staff put up a small stage, and Geshe Michael came there blindfolded, along with the other retreatants, so as not to interrupt their solitude. Students sat on blankets in the sand of the wash, on our side of the retreat boundary. The teachings went from evening into the night, and as the sun went down the dry desert air went from warm to very cold, and the moon rose full in the sky over our little group.

We'd sit quietly waiting for the teachings to begin, listening to the late afternoon song of the desert. As the retreatants were led out to the teaching area, many of us burst into tears. Over a year into the retreat, it felt as if their very presence was filled now with the profound heartfelt depth of meditative solitude.

From Geshe-hla, we heard that to find our perfect teacher we needed to be those highest qualities for others. We heard how the world is sprinkled with divine beings whose mission is to teach us in our daily life. The consideration, generosity and tenderness with which people treated each other mushroomed. We started looking at each other quizzically, as if wondering, "Could *you* be one who came into this world to teach me?" It was hard to say goodbye at the end of the teachings. Many small kindnesses may have been forgotten, but gratitude remained—especially towards our Teacher, who had given us much to practice until we gathered together again.

So as you read, imagine you are sitting with friends in the cool stillness of a moonlit desert night, listening to your teacher, your old friend, as he tries to convey his experiences and his understandings—to give you a taste of what his retreat is like, and to pass on something that will be of benefit to your life. The moment is precious; he has only a short time to tell you everything he wants you to know, and then he will go back for another six months of quiet, and you will go back to your family, to your job in the city far away from this place. At the beginning of each evening's teaching is a short verse, or you could say a root text, around which the teaching would be formed. You can use these verses later to remember, perhaps taking them into your own retreat, to contemplate the thoughts behind them and try to make them your own. This is what these teachings are for and that is what this book is for.

It is incredibly rare to receive teachings from a Teacher immersed in deep retreat, and our intention is to share the special wisdom and blessings of these unique teachings with you as freshly and powerfully as they came to us. For that reason, editing has been kept to a minimum, to preserve the expression of his solitude and realizations.

First Day:

Thursday, March 8, 2001

We need the perfect Teacher

I.

Imagine the concert hall without one.
The blessing of living touch;
Instant depth, tricks and pitfalls,
Generations to the beginning.

A companion for life,
And like-minded friends;
Entry to a new world
Of people, places, and tools.

Someone to take you
Outside, beneath, and beyond yourself.
Don't be afraid to fish for the best;
Hook them with your service.

But first be clear
That what you want to learn
Is what They teach,
Or the marriage will never last.

In a world created
Moment to moment by imprints,
You master all things
By mastering one:

Serving others;
The high hard art of serving others.

Nothing for yourself;
Not even "I come to learn to serve,"
But rather "I come to serve and learn."
A relief to hear it said.

Learn to serve others
With a thousand hands,
From trifles
To deathlessness.

First I'd like to meditate for a few minutes.

We've been in retreat now, last weekend was the first year, and looking back, it seems like many strange coincidences, a long string of them, have occurred. Maybe twenty years ago, the greatest Lama began introducing American people to a very holy secret practice from Tibet. Many years later, Pabongka Rinpoche the Third handed one of us a book and said, "Maybe you'll need this." And then five or six amazing people started to come to class in New York.

We were crossing Second Avenue one day—it's pretty big—and stepping off the sidewalk someone said, "How about three year retreat?" And before we reached the next sidewalk on the other side, it was decided.

Then strangely we started to get insistent letters from a lady in Arizona whom I'd never heard of. We must come and see a land near a mountain. We came on a free day from Tucson, and we met a holy man posing as a rancher and a builder, and—by coincidence—he had walked on the grounds of Sera Monastery in Tibet and admired the debate ground.

Then, coincidentally, a great woman from holy Lama Zopa Rinpoche's group, one of his finest students, appeared to help us. Then by coincidence, we were in Mongolia and right next to the library where we were working was a huge yurt display lot, and they would love to send some to America.

And by great coincidence a holy Mongolian man, posing as a normal person, was available to arrange shipping of them, which is not allowed, from Mongolia. And by coincidence, there was a holy woman posing as a mom [laughter] who'd been waiting thirty years for the yurts, took care of everything—shipping and unpacking these huge crates.

And, by coincidence, there was a holy man posing as a normal student in California who drove them here. And at the same time, by total sheer coincidence, there was a group of three or four people in New York who had nothing to do for the month, and would love to drive all our boxes of junk out so we could throw them away here [laughter].

And then, by sheer coincidence, a group of holy beings posing as people who have an extra month or two to fry themselves in the sun here, built the beautiful yurts for us, while we were over sleeping in our tents in the park.

And by coincidence a gentle man, posing as a businessman and professor, had an extra three or four years to sell his house and move all his family here, to take care of everything.

And then, by sheer coincidence, there was a child psychologist who worked in religious schools who was willing to come and take care of us, because we are like that [laughter].

Then, by coincidence, there was an extremely energetic young lady who had trained to fix meals and nurse people who were ill, and she said, "I'm not doing anything for three years. I'll help cook and take care of you."

And then, by sheer coincidence, there was a woman who had spent many years of her life working in a post office and saving the money, and she would like to give it and give her life's time to help manage all of this caretaking.

All by coincidence.

And by coincidence there are many holy people, a doctor whom we knew in New York moved to Tucson—by coincidence—at the same time to take care of us. Many coincidences like that.

You people must be careful. Even stupid people like us can figure it out [laughter], if you do it too often. Don't expose your identities. Try to be more normal.

They say that if you see emptiness directly for fifteen or twenty minutes, even if you come close, that you have done a greater thing than all the good things in your life up to then. Thirty, forty years of trying to do little good things, eclipsed in less than a half an hour. Enough goodness created during that brief time, I think if you changed it to electricity or something, you could create the planet you're sitting on. Enough goodness to create countless millions of tons of matter that whole civilizations can live on for thousands of years, created in a few minutes. They that say you need to meditate deeply, quietly, for at least six months or a year, to have a chance to see these things.

And so it seems the kindest thing a person could ever do for us is to give us that chance, or at least a hope to come close. I think you may not realize what you are doing for us. I think you may not understand how much you have given us. It is the greatest gift that a person could give to another person, to give them the chance [cries]. I don't think we could thank you. It's obvious to all of us that all we can do is try very hard to do what we are here to do. You should know that everyone tries so hard; they have spent a long hard year.

We were walking home one day from prayers together, which now we only do about every third month, and someone waved their arm towards the mountain and the yurts in a way that we knew meant, "It looks so peaceful." And we all laughed, because inside those yurts it is like Vietnam or World War One [laughter]. It's hard work in the trenches, and bombs going off, and shots overhead. Long hours. Winter was hard. Winter was cold, although people did their best to make us warm.

It was dark; many hours of darkness. The yurts are dark. We don't have any electricity; only one person has solar. We spent long hours in the darkness, in the cold, and meditating. It was hard. And so you should be proud of the retreatants. They have not complained; they have not given up. They have had hard days of doubt and loneliness and they have persevered. And they are flowering inside, as spring comes.

4

I would like to speak about teachers.

Sometimes you get a feeling that you would like to learn something new. You might see an extraordinary person—maybe a musician who plays extraordinary music, and then your heart leaps inside and you say, "I want to learn to do that. I want to learn to do it as well as they do."

Then maybe you try. You go and buy a flute in the store and after you sit for a few hours, it becomes clear you can't even make it peep. And then, especially if you are very serious to become a master, you set out to find a true teacher. Anyone who tries to learn something great realizes at some point they must find a master teacher *[crying]*.

There's a blessing to a living person that can never be even approximated by books or tapes or videos. There's a blessing to how a great musician holds their arms, or how they walk, how they sit, how they look around the room, how they speak, how they touch their instrument so lovingly. None of these things can be taught in a book; you have to be at their side. You learn greatness only by being at their side. And it's not, I think, so much what they teach you but how they are that infects you and grows inside you. There's nothing like it—you can't play piano in a great concert hall unless a master has guided you for many years.

I think those of you who have mastered anything—building, painting, music, anything—you did it only because of the kindness of a living person. There's a blessing that comes from their hands when they touch you, when they put their hand over your hand on the piano, and they show you how to do it, how to touch the key. There's a blessing that has come from many generations, through living hands touching each other, from master to student for generations. I think truly, when a master piano teacher touches his or her student's hand, there's a magical blessing coming down, from the first days that piano was ever played, because it has passed down through living hands. There's nothing like it.

If you learn from a great master from the beginning, even just how to push the keys down properly, you never learn anything wrong, and you don't have to be re-taught again later. If the first time you heard the Heart Sutra chanted was by the greatest abbot of Sera Mey who ever lived, then it just enters you in that holy way the first time, with an instant depth of many generations that you could never reach by yourself.

Master teachers teach you the pitfalls. They say, "If you want to do this move right in this dance, never point your toe that way and then turn. You'll break it."

You don't have to break it; they warn you in advance. They give you guidance that saves you much pain, maybe years of the pain of doing something the wrong way. From the first day, they show you tricks. You're learning yoga, and they say, "Oh, if you can't do that, just move this way," and suddenly you can do it. You never would have figured it out. Many things are like that. You need a master close by.

When you find a real master there's a special comfort. If you are intense, if you are devoted with your whole heart to any subject—it could be piano, it could be painting, it could be dance, it could be building things—then suddenly you have found your family. Not your blood family, but the family of the heart. You have a lifelong companion now. If you are learning racecar driving, you suddenly have someone that you can sit and drink tea with and talk about racecars all night, for life. If you meet a real master you have met a companion for life, a companion of the heart.

If you meet a real master, then they often have already great disciples, great talented students. And suddenly you have a family to live with; people who are as odd as you are, who have the same strange interest in a single thing. Suddenly you are among a whole new family of people who are like you and they teach you as much as the master teaches you.

When you find a real master, suddenly you enter a whole different world. They know everywhere to go; they know everyone who is close; they have resources. They say, "You want to see that piece played properly? Come tonight, there's a man I know playing it in his home."

"Come to this special hall where they're rehearsing. I know the director; you can see the play done by great masters."

These are almost like a mandala, like a secret world. When you meet a real master, suddenly the door is open to you. You meet many people who are masters; you are taken to unbelievable places where the masters meet together quietly. The master will pull out a book or a score of music and say, "This is something my teacher gave me; no one has seen it. Try this one."

And they know. They have these special tools, special resources for you. You can't find those on the web. You can't learn those on your own; it has to come from a living master. When you go to a real master, then something happens. They become your mirror. They are outside of you. When you practice something by yourself, if you try to master something without a master, you can't see yourself. You make many mistakes that you can't see. Sometimes it's just because your foot is behind your back—you can't see it. And sometimes it's because we don't want to see our mistakes, and it takes a holy master to correct us.

For a lifetime, a great master and a great disciple enter into a relationship of correction. This is what masters are for. This is what master teachers do. By agreeing to that relationship, the students have humbly opened themselves to constant and often painful correction. This is impossible by yourself. You can't become a master by yourself, because you can't see yourself. The master stands outside you and corrects what are obvious faults to the whole world, except to yourself. So a master has the quality of helping you.

To go to a teacher and to humbly ask to be taught is an act of humility. We are all too proud; we are all too sure that we are good and right. But when you go to a teacher and you ask to be taught, then by nature you are admitting that there are things that he or she knows better, and you are dealing a great blow to the pride that prevents you from becoming a master. So to go to a master, in the first moment is a great act of humility, which we all lack, and even in the first moment it makes you a stronger person. It enables you to grow into a master, because the greater the master, the more they know they are not so great.

I think lastly, a master takes you beyond yourself. How many times have you observed this in a class? I think of a yoga class, and the teacher stands with a wristwatch and says, "Hold this for two minutes on one leg." And you are sweating at one minute, and you are shaking at two minutes, and then they say, "Let's see if you can do five." And you can't believe it; you are shaking.

I have watched one of the greatest masters of yoga in the world teaching a student from another country. The student was on the floor, and he said, "Go down further."

And she said, "I can't."

And he said, "Do it."

7

And she said, "I can't."

And he said, "You will!"

And he got on top of her with about two hundred pounds and crushed her to the floor.

And I heard "AH! AH! AH!"

And then about two minutes later she walked out of the room and her face was radiant, gleaming with pride that she had gone far beyond what she could do before.

Only a master can take you far beyond the place where you would have given up long before *[cries]*.

And so I think when you want to learn something, which we all do, you should go for the best. Find the greatest master, hold out for the perfect teacher, and don't be satisfied with less. Don't be afraid to approach the greatest.

I have a friend who is a very talented moviemaker. I said, "How did you learn these things?"

She said, "There's a great director. I went to him and said, 'Will you teach me?'"

He said, "I have no time, and you couldn't afford it."

And she said, "I'll become your servant. I will run for coffee, I will make the phone calls, I will go to the grocery store. Just let me hang out near you."

And he said, "OK."

So great masters are like big fish, you have to hook them. The way to hook them is with service.

Be like the camel and the tent. "Just let me put my foot in your tent; it's cold outside." And then by midnight the whole leg is in. By two o'clock the front part is in, kind of smelling funny, and then by morning you are sleeping with a camel.

So don't be afraid. Seriously. Find a great master; go for the highest. Your life is short. You have something to learn. You have to learn to become a master yourself. You can only do it by being close to a great master.

In my experience most great masters need someone to help them. Even His Holiness, the sweet Holy Dalai Lama, doesn't have enough people near him to help. If you ever have a chance to be near him or any other great person for a few days, you would realize there are not many students who are wise enough to come and throw themselves at the masters' feet and serve them to gain priceless wisdom.

But I have seen also people come and throw themselves at the feet of great masters. I lived with the greatest master for over twenty fortunate years *[crying]*. I saw many people come, and I saw most of them fail, and only recently I realized why. What they wanted to learn or to become was not what the master was teaching. And it took sometimes years for both parties to realize it.

They appeared to be true students but, in the end, they didn't really want to learn what the master was teaching. They wanted something different. So I think first it's important to decide what is it you want to learn, because you may go to the wrong master. I'm thinking of a great concert pianist, and a person goes to them and begs them to teach them to be a master. They sit down at the piano and the student says, "What's this?"

And the master says, "It's the piano; this is what I am the master of."

And they say, "No, I wanted to learn bongos."

And the master says, "I don't teach bongos; I'm a piano master."

However in the field of spiritual things, it takes sometimes a long time before they find out the person wanted bongos, not piano.

I think it's important to understand one thing. Lord Buddha's greatest teaching was that the entire world around us, every single object you see, is a creation of your mind. It doesn't mean you can't touch it; of course you can touch things. It doesn't mean you can't get killed by a moving vehicle; of course you can be. But it means that the way you see things—the way you see a car, or a desert bush, or the sky, or your own thoughts—are all determined, are all dictated, by your mind. You form images from moment to moment. It's happening so smoothly, like a smooth computer video, that you can't even catch yourself.

That's why we are meditating. When you meditate deeply, you can catch it, because the frames slow down. So instant to instant, moment to moment, the entire mass of the world around you with its billions of tons of earth, thousands of people, and countless stars, are all images formed within your mind. Everything is an image formed inside your mind. And whether it is something good or bad, whether it is something that makes you happy or not, the content of the images and forms is solely determined by your behavior towards other people in the past. No good thing has ever occurred to a living creature on this earth in its history unless they had done something very similar for someone else in the past. No evil has ever existed on this planet or any other planet unless the person who suffers from that evil did the same evil to someone else. And there's no beginning.

So everything comes from how we treat others. If you go to a piano master, and if they teach you and you learn well, it is only because you spoke sweetly to others in the past. It has nothing to do with anything else. If you go to a teacher—yoga, tai chi, or something—to make yourself healthy, and you succeed and you feel strong energy in your body, it is only because you served the sick and avoided harming life in the past. It has nothing to do with the yoga. If you go to study a language or a philosophy, and you suddenly understand it easily—it pours into you like an ocean—it is only because you have provided that wisdom to others in the past yourself. Because they are all images in your mind.

You can't see a healthy body, you can't hear a heartbreaking song, you can't think a holy thought, unless you have provided others with the same in the past, because these are only images created by the same mind that helped others in the past.

I think to take a break now. Please enjoy some refreshments. Get a sweater or a jacket, and we'll do a little more after that. Okay?

So, if you try to learn anything, if you try to become a master of anything and you succeed, if some kind of exercise makes you strong, if you find yourself able to play beautiful music, if you open a Dharma book and understanding floods into your mind, these are all only images created by your mind. The music is only some vibrations. The strong body is only some colors. The understanding is only some sounds in a mind. It is your past actions towards others which organize these random sounds and shapes and thoughts into success. It is only by serving others that these images can come in your mind, and they are reality. They are very real, *because* they are images.

So any person listening to this who has the mental images to be intelligent, would think now, "Oh, then I should learn to serve others, because then I can succeed at anything." And that's true. You have to find a master of serving others.

People come and say, "I want to learn Tibetan." No, we don't teach that here.

People say, "I want to learn philosophy." No, we don't teach that here.

People say, "I want to learn to meditate." We don't even teach that here.

"I want to learn to do retreats." We don't teach that here. Go somewhere else.

"I want to learn secret tantra." We don't teach that here.

"I want to see emptiness." We don't even teach that here.

The student must first clearly realize that what they want to learn is what's being taught, and no great master who understood emptiness and images would teach anything less than the source of all happiness, which is only serving others, doing nothing for yourself, only for others, because they're empty.

"Then I want to come to learn to serve others."

You already made a mistake in your words. No, you come here to serve others. Say it like that. The "serve others" has to come first, before the learning.

"Oh, do you mean I have to wash dishes for a year?" No, you have to serve others first. Your reason to come to this dry hot place, cold place, in your mind you have to have only one hope and one idea—to serve others—not even to learn.

So there's a difference between learning to serve, and serving and learning. It's not the same. In your mind, first before all, if you understand emptiness and images, the real source of all happiness is only helping and serving others.

11

"Oh thank you. I heard you; I'll go and cook meals for poor people, and go to hospitals and take care of sick people."

No, it's not that easy. Serving others is a high art, a higher art than any classical art. It takes decades of your life to learn the high art of serving others. It's hard to serve others.

From the beginning it's almost impossible to overcome our attachment to our own happiness, which is a great poison, a cancer that spreads throughout our world and kills the happiness of humanity. If things are empty, if everything around you is an image of your mind planted in the past by how you treated others, then there's no choice: you must serve others. Nothing good can ever happen unless you take care of others.

If you go to a Lama, and they say to you, "No, I'm not teaching Tibetan language; I'm not teaching books; I'm not teaching rituals; I'm not teaching meditation or retreats; I'm not teaching how to be a monk or nun. I'm only teaching how to serve people. Then if you are *kelwa sangpo,* if you are a person of incredible good fortune, your heart leaps to hear it said. We teach serving others. You feel a chill up your spine. You start to cry. Finally I found someone who is teaching the right thing. And your heart knows that's true. So when you come here to learn, you must think only, "I'm coming to serve." It's such a relief to hear someone say it.

How to serve? Oh, you have to grow nine hundred and ninety eight new arms and hands. You must have a thousand hands. Those aren't just silly pictures of Holy Dalai Lama Chenrezig. Those are true. You need a thousand arms. You have to learn the high art of serving others.

Holiest Lama Khen Rinpoche used to say, "Go down in the basement and watch the repairman fix the furnace."

I'd say, "I came here to learn philosophy. I came here to become a master."

"Shut up and go down in the basement and watch the man fix the furnace. Learn how to do it. You can serve others."

"The Kalmuks are coming today for a funeral, three hundred of them. They want *mo-mo*s. They want meat dumplings."

12

"I don't eat meat."

"You will cut the meat by hand and you will make the dough by hand and you will serve them until your fingers are raw. And while I am in India, can you build me a house?"

And you say, "I didn't come to do that, I came to learn Buddhism."

And he says, "No, you came to here to learn to serve others, but you have to grow a thousand arms."

Not everyone wants to learn emptiness. Not everyone wants to hear about images in their mind. Some people just want a cup of coffee. And you have to serve them. Once a student said to holy Lama Geshe Ngawang Dhargye, who has left this world, "I don't want to make coffee for people. It's suffering. Coffee is just a short worldly pleasure, and it goes away. It even hurts the people who want it."

And Geshe Dhargye said, "You are a fool. You have to learn to serve everyone what they want, from small stupid harmful things up to deathlessness itself."

You must grow a thousand arms. You have to learn everything. Watch anyone doing anything. How to make a nice meal. How to fix a car. How to use a hammer. Don't be a fool and say I only serve emptiness. You have to learn to serve everything, because the living beings you are serving have vastly different hopes and wishes. If you ever hope to bring them beyond the demon of death, you must learn to make them happy in small ways first. And then slowly they will follow you higher. But you need to know all of these ways of serving others first.

So let this place become school of serving others. And warn people who come here. We don't teach bongos; we teach serving others. And if they will agree, without hesitation, to learn to serve others, then slowly they must be gifted the knowledge of dishwashing, and then hammering, and then the knowledge of the holy books, and then meditation, and then retreat, and then the mysteries of the secret teachings. And one by one, serve them up more and more holy dishes.

Thank you so much for coming here. It's a hard trip, I know. It's hard to find time. And thank you so much for helping the sincere people who are in retreat here. It's a holy marriage of sweet-minded people who want to help and sweet-minded people who want to try to reach something that will serve many people. It's like a sun shining in this small place, a few people in the world, very precious and rare, meeting of good intentions and holy thoughts. I think we can all be happy. I hope we can serve others.

Second Day:

Friday, March 9, 2001

What makes the perfect Teacher?

II.

Find and become the perfect Teacher:
A Grandmaster with a big toolbox,
An open bag of candy,
A desert dandelion, and the air we breathe;

Stainless steel; a sculptor
Of every stone, with a master plan;
A mother bird
With a single motive.

Rocket fuel, and a match;
An echo, a taskmaster
Correcting and driving
With carrot and stick.

A gas pedal, a general
With the orders, a pillow,
An ant with winter coming,
Branching tunnels ready.

A chameleon on
The same old rock,
A lawn of grass,
An old temple gong.

Pruning shears
For a fresh sapling,
Mount Meru and
A rubber ball.

A teacher of learning and teaching;
And learning, teaching, an honor.
A builder glad to go to first grade
Even in their own school.

A proud poppa,
A push from the nest,
Genghis Khan and lieutenants,
A maker and passer of the torch.

A spider in a big web,
Peer revelry,
A free referral service;
A piggy bank, teddy bear, bureaucrat.

A golden magnet,
Symphony conductor,
An old pair of shoes
And an old hat.

An active player
By their own gameplan;
A kid single-pointed
On a double-scoop cone.

A gem carver,
A new edition of an old book,

Triple evolution,
Trail blazer and lion.

A golden retriever
And a koala bear,
Gold to file or cut or melt,
A scientist and detective.

A word to the wise,
A ballerina
One or two gathered
Or in the arena.

A seal
In a quiet sea,
A match
Made in heaven.

I'd like to meditate for a few minutes.

People asked us when we went into retreat, "What will you do when you come out?" And you can imagine we spoke about it together at great length. And then finally we felt that it was better to have no plan, because we felt that we should be ready to do whatever wonderful great thing we would see was good for other people during our retreat. We thought that during the three years some higher instructions might come, and we wanted to be sure to be available and free for them. And so we stripped away the things that reminded us of what we had been. Our clothes changed and many other things, and we even asked the kind dakinis who care for us not to address us by our old names. We each have a symbol, like a star or a moon, and that's how they send us a message.

It reminds me of reading about a fisherman, two brothers who are just fishing. A strange man they've never met comes up and says, "Come with me. I'll make you fishers of men, instead of fish." And amazingly, they drop their career and their life in the middle of the morning, and walk off with nothing.

17

We have each a small bag near the door of Cheerios and warm socks, in case somebody taps us on the shoulder during meditation and says "Come for something higher." And even walking here blindfolded with a holy being holding each of our hands, we try to think maybe they are taking me to the platform, or maybe they are leading me to a cliff and we will both fly off together. It would be nice. So I think it's important for each of us here to be free in this way: available for a higher call all the time.

That having been said, and one year having passed, I would like to remind you of some agreements we had. Four of them are outside agreements and four of them are inside agreements.

The first one is that some kind people said they would try to go through all of the translations we had, and connect the Tibetan words with the English words so that people in the future could translate the hundreds of thousands of extraordinary, sacred, holy books from Tibet. One person said he'd try to make it happen. He didn't know a lot about that idea, and very bravely—he didn't know Tibetan. If that person is here, or the person who may have come up in his place if he's not doing it anymore, if that person is here, please stand up. [Ted Lemon stands up.] I don't see the future clearly, but I feel threads of what might come, and one thread is in his hand, and you must try to help him or her.

That's the first. You can sit down if you're here. But don't be shy to approach him and offer your help: that's why he's standing.

The second thread I sense is we have a list of several thousand important, mostly secret books that must be saved. And one kind man, who also wasn't very familiar with the work that had gone before, offered to try to have things done. If he's here, or she—whoever may have replaced him—please stand. [John Brady stands up]. [Crying.] You must try to help this person. They have almost impossible job to do, and what they are trying to do must be done in this world. Those things must not be lost. Okay, sit down if you are here.

Third thing. I feel it's very important for the future that there be a large space near a mountain, where we can sprinkle many holy beings retreating in small places far from each other, trying to reach ultimate happiness for everyone. One man, who has a thousand other holy responsibilities, agreed to try to arrange that, as far as possible. This is very difficult task—may not be possible—but we should try to do that or something similar. That person should stand up, or whoever is doing that job now. [Winston McCullough stands up.] Try to help him. I think it can only be done by a number of the most intelligent and resourceful people here—you know who you are—working together with very great. You have to think hard of special ways to do something that's hard to do.

And then the fourth outer task that I feel may be important is that as many people as possible must try to finish the eighteen courses of this school, so they are ready to go on to the higher course which is appearing. And especially in a big city in the East Coast. Can that man or whoever has replaced him stand up? [John Stilwell stands up.]

You must try to help him, and you must try to encourage as many people as possible to be ready. Events will move swiftly and strongly, and sometimes in a frightening way, and we need people to be ready. It may not be something that will come twice—they must be ready. Also in other places like a big island below Japan, Bonny Doon, and Santa Cruz, people must be ready.

People who have the ability to teach others must organize things for others and push them along. There are only two years left now; you should be finished with six courses. Anyone you feel might be ready for the higher teachings, you must take responsibility for them; they don't know enough to be ready. You have to encourage them and urge them to be ready.

Oh, you can sit down. Especially if you're here. If you're still you. Help him or her, in your respective places. Also of course, needless to say, people here must be most ready.

The inner agreement first was, especially for the leaders who are taking holy hlaksam nyamdak—personal responsibility—for others. Those people agreed, many of them swore, to do two long retreats per year each.

I never read letters from outside, but sometimes I can guess what's going on. I see a corner of a note that says, "So and so is in retreat; they can't cook you your Indian meal today." So I have sensed that many people are doing retreat and I thank you for that holy thing. Even people who had many things to do just before this teaching did the best thing; they locked themselves up for a month.

The second inner agreement was that each of those people who take responsibility, you must continue your studies yourself. It's not good to be teaching other people and leading them, and not take care that you yourself are finishing the eighteen courses and studying every day.

The third inner agreement we had was that each person would do deep meditation one to one-and-a-half hours per day. You cannot help another person without that. Don't fall into the trap of serving the Dharma and not doing your meditation. You can't help
anyone without that.

The fourth agreement we had was that each person, every hour-and-a-half or two, would forcefully tear themselves away from their work and write down the condition of their heart at that moment and how well they have kept their vows in the last two hours. If I could see you in my meditation, if I had the power, would I see a spotty book, or would I see a full book? Would there be nice full pages, or would there be skipped pages? It's not for myself or for anyone else; it's the only way to clean your own mind and help other people.

The last thing about these things is that each one is less important than the next. If you haven't done your book, don't start your meditation. If you haven't done your book and your meditation then don't open the course book to study. If you haven't done your book, and your meditation and your study, don't think retreat is going to help much.

It's the same with the outer four. After you have finished the inner four, if you have time, then try to help others learn the courses. Once it's assured that others are learning, then you can take any extra time and help try to find a place where we can place many meditators. If you have assured that people are learning, and if you have helped as much as you can to find a place for future meditators, then work on saving the books. And if all others are healthy and strong, then take some time to translate or help to create tools to translate. Those are the priorities. They are very clear.

If you are a working person and busy most of the day, then whatever time you have left you should divide into two equal parts for meditation and study, with meditation first. If you are a person who is serving the Dharma all day as a teacher or as a careperson, then for every two hours you spend on other things like study, you should spend one hour meditating. Those are the priorities, those are very clear.

We spoke yesterday about what a huge difference there is between trying to learn something yourself and having a master teacher at your side guiding your hand. There's no comparison. We said that one reason, I think, why some students fail is that they come to the teacher for the wrong reasons. They don't really intend or want to learn what that teacher is teaching. They have another agenda in their heart, and then sooner or later the relationship breaks down.

Then we said that if the world is empty, like a white screen, and if everything you have ever laid your eyes upon is an image created by your own past behavior towards other people, then what you really should do is to try to learn as well as you can is to serve other people. If every experience you ever had came directly from something you did to someone else before, if no object in your world around you affects another object, then gasoline doesn't make cars go; food doesn't make people go; teachers don't even make students learn.

Everything comes from your own mind; everything comes from seeds planted there before when you were either kind or unkind to others. Try to grasp the monumental significance of this idea. Nothing makes other things go at all. No word or gesture or touch of the hand between people causes anything in another person. Everything is flowing from a different source. Everything is flowing from what you did to others in the past. Only a fool would try to learn something other than serving others, because no matter what you undertake, its success is only assured by images that flow into your mind from imprints planted when you were kind or unkind to others. If you understand emptiness, if you understand that the world doesn't work any other way, you should thirst to become a master of serving others.

And so today I thought, we'll do something almost like fun—we rarely have fun; perhaps when we get out [of retreat]. You have a list, I hope, in your hands, of the qualities of a perfect teacher. There are great lists in holy books about the qualities of a Buddhist master, both open and secret masters. But I thought we'd just make a list of qualities of any teacher: of piano, or art, or architecture, or dance, or a teacher of anything. The qualities that I think we all admire in a teacher.

The list has two functions. One is to help you in your search for a perfect teacher of the ultimate skill, which is serving others. It's not easy. Serving others is not as

21

simple as it looks. It takes years of training from a great master. I'm not saying a Buddhist master; I'm saying from a person who truly knows how to serve others, from small ways like food, up to the highest ways, like not having to die. So this is a list for looking for this kind of teacher, or for any teacher. And it's also a list for each of us to aspire to. These are the qualities I think most of them you will agree we must each develop if we are to serve others. And that is the only intelligent thing to do with your lifetime.

I will go through the first few that I remember, and then at some point when my old brain fails, I'll say, "What's the next one?" Then please don't be shy even if you're in the back, just yell it out, "The next one is…whatever." This will go a little late maybe, so be patient. It's not much to get cold for one evening if it means you can learn to serve the living creatures that are walking or crawling on millions of planets. You can keep count and mark it on the page. I think there are ninety-something qualities.

The first quality I think naturally we would all look for that is they should know what the heck they're talking about. They should be very good at what they do. They should know what they are talking about. Don't be satisfied with less. Don't be polite. Find the master, find the person who is really the best in the world at what they do. Your life is at stake. You're spending your holy precious few years of adult health; don't waste your holy time.

They should have a big toolbox. For example, a piano teacher should know how to play Mozart, and Bach, and Tchaikovsky, and Rachmaninoff, and they should have a huge vocabulary. They should know many different masters' work. Secondly, they should have depth in each of them. Some masters are masters in depth of only one thing. Some people are masters of many things, but nothing in depth. You are looking to find—and you are looking to become—a master who knows many great methods of doing what they do, and they are very good at each of them. That's **a grand master with a big toolbox**.

I hope I didn't forget the second already. What's the second? [**An open bowl of candy.**]

It's no good to find a master who doesn't like to teach. You can imagine many masters: they are grumpy, eccentric masters, and they say, "I don't have time to teach. I'm not interested in teaching anyone." There are other kinds of grumpy masters who say, "I'll teach you a little." But they withhold the very most precious things.

"Open" means they give you their all. They give you everything. They don't hold back anything; they pour it into you. And "bowl of candy" means they would love you to come and learn and take what they know. They want you to come and take what they know.

What's the next one? **Desert Dandelion**. You may have met them, and if you haven't you will. They are little yellow-stemmed plants, a few inches high, growing mostly near the oak trees, and they have black spikes that go out like a dandelion. On the end of the spike are three little hooks. You walk innocently under the oaks and, if a rattlesnake doesn't bite you, these dandelions sprinkle you with these little sticky things. They're not like thorns; they're just straight little straw-like things. When you get home and sit down on your meditation seat, suddenly your bottom is pierced by ten or twenty, and then you spend the next half hour of your precious time pulling them out.

The idea is that the transmission is perfect; it's so smooth and seamless. You just walk along and they cover you without you knowing it. A great master must not only know everything, they must not only be willing to teach you, but they must know how to teach. The delivery system must be perfect. It's no good if they are knowledgeable, and it's no good if they want to teach if they can't teach, if they don't speak your language—meaning they won't transmit to you in a very smooth way.

The air we breathe means there may be a master who is very good at what they do. They may wish to teach you, and they may be a good teacher. But they must be like the air around us. It's available all the time. You just suck, and it comes in. It's around you constantly. And I think in the case of great masters, oftentimes they are just not available. They're busy, or they're traveling, or they have many responsibilities. And so regardless of what qualities they may have, it doesn't matter if they are not available. If you can't be with them or if they haven't made some plan for making someone available to you, then it doesn't matter.

In the old diamond company my truly holy boss, Ofer, and I used to evaluate people for raises. Someone's name would come up, and we would say, "This person is intelligent, this person is a good team player; this person is talented; this person produces."

And he would say, "How's their attendance?"
And I'd say, "Well, they're absent a lot."

And he'd say, "Well, what the heck does it matter, if they don't show up?" So a master must be available.

Next is? **Stainless steel.** I think a teacher of any subject should have integrity, even if you are learning business, or piano, or sports. If someone is your business mentor and you find out they are cheating a customer, then you get discouraged. You don't want to learn from them. The same in music: if you found out that a person was cheating a student. Or in sports. In sports I remember a great coach losing it one day and punching a player from the opposite team who had made a good play, a college student. Then immediately you don't feel like being with this master.

A master should be clean of any scandal or problems like that, integrity problems. We expose ourselves to a master—we are vulnerable to a teacher—and if they are not pure, if they don't have integrity, then even in things like sports we don't feel like we want to learn from them. They should have integrity.

Teachers should be like **a master sculpture of every stone, with a master plan**. *Heh! [Laughter.]*

When a perspective student walks into a school of a master, the master should look at them, and after talking with them and seeing what they can do, they should have a vision of what they can make this person into. Holy Lama Khen Rinpoche went to Italy with holy Lama Art, and when they came home Rinpoche repeatedly talked about Michelangelo. He said, "I understood how he looked at a piece of marble and he saw what was inside. He was only exposing what was already there in his mind."

And a great teacher should size up a student, even in the first few days, and they should have a vision of what this person could become, even exceeding whatever small vision the student may have. The master should look at them and say, "I can make something beautiful from this stone."

Someone might say, "That's lousy stone. That's not marble, that's some kind of cheap imitation stone. This student doesn't have much aptitude." And a master teacher should say, "I don't care about that, I can make a masterpiece from any stone. I see even in the poorest stone a holy, sacred, beautiful being"

And so I think great masters of anything are willing to take on a student, if they are sincere, and make them into something great, no matter how rough the material to start. I think a master teacher should have a master plan. 'First I will do this with this student. A year from now, I will do this. Three years from now, I will tell them about this. Five years from now, I will introduce them to something bigger.' They should have in the back of their minds a twenty or thirty year plan for this person, until they have perfected the statue.

What's next? **Mother bird with a single motive.** I think **single motive** comes first—a true teacher of anything should have a single thing in mind, which is making this student a master, giving them what they wish, making their dreams come true. This should be their only motive. They should look at this person's hopes to become very good at something, and say, "I will make their wishes come true. I will make this person truly happy." Not those other sick motives, like, "I'll become famous if I have many students." "I can get money or other material things from this person." "I can fulfill my emotional needs by having this person near me." "I can fulfill my physical needs by having them near me." "I can use this person for my projects." Not like that. The teacher must look at them and have a single idea: "I want to fulfill this person's dreams."

A **mother bird** would go further. When a mother bird comes with a worm, they don't eat it first; they give the first part to their child. And a great master who is truly great should choose the happiness of their student even before their own. If someone comes to them and says, "There's a chance to have an interview with Time magazine," or "There's a chance to play a concert tonight at Carnegie Hall," and if they have made a commitment to their student, they would say, "I'm busy." *[Cries]*. The student comes first.

Another meaning of **mother** is that a teacher should have social conscience. I think most great teachers of any subject, for example piano, you may often find them doing a charity concert. They want to use what they know to bring happiness to others. I think that's a sign of a true master teacher.

When holy Lama Khen Rinpoche *[crying]* came to this strange land, he didn't have a nickel. He didn't know anybody. He couldn't speak the language of the people around him and he was already almost sixty. How could he have a hope to do anything? But he saved his nickels and dimes, and he is feeding every single of the almost two thousand monks of Sera Mey Monastery. He never spends anything on himself. There's a sign of a master teacher.

What's the next one? **Rocket fuel and a match.** We spoke briefly yesterday about what **rocket fuel** means. A master teacher takes you beyond what you could do yourself. They push you; they push your envelope far beyond what you could ever hope to do for yourself. A master of anything pushes the student beyond. They have the vision of what this person could become if they were pushed. It hurts sometimes, but you have to do it. It's a great kindness. And the student normally bucks them; the student normally resists. "I can't do that." Either they say it or they think it. And it's hard to push a student beyond what they think their limits are. It takes a great deal of trust and love and faith between a student and a master to allow the master to push you, to propel you beyond what you thought you could do.

A **match** means somebody who lights your fire. I heard a flute player, Emer Mayock, from Ireland. I heard one or two songs, and I told Christie-hla, "I'm going to quit everything and become a flute player. I need to learn to play like that." But I was too busy *[laughs]*.

A true teacher should inspire you. You look at them and say, "I want to learn that. I need to learn that." They should put a fire in your heart that may need to last for decades. "I want to be like that."

What's the next one? **An echo.** Holy Lama Ofer Azrielant of Andin International used to call me in and say, "Did you review this person's performance today?"

I'd say, "I was busy the whole month."

He would get angry. He'd say, "Imagine you're in a bowling alley. Someone comes and says, 'You roll those balls hard down that ramp, as hard as you can. I want you to roll one every ten or twenty seconds.' And then they walk down to the pins and they cover them with a sheet." He said, "It's hard to keep rolling the balls if you don't know if you hit anything. You get tired; you want to know how you're doing."

A great teacher must constantly help the student know, "How am I doing? Am I going okay? Am I doing the right thing?" They must set up a system by which the student is constantly reviewed, constantly told, "Yes this thing you are doing very well; this thing not so good—you have to improve."

A great teacher must be like an echo; they must get back to you with feedback about how you're doing. They must also require some kind of work that you do on your own, that you bring back to them. They say, "By Thursday, you must learn to do these three moves with your right foot, I'm going to check."

And then they must check. If you don't check, the student becomes discouraged: "They don't care." So a great teacher must be like an echo.

What's the next? **Correcting and driving with a carrot and stick.**

I think we'd better have refreshments before carrot and stick. [Laughter.] Let's take a break. [Break]

The reason we go to a master to learn is that we hope to be corrected. When we don't make a move so well, or play a song right, we are going to them expressly for the purpose of being corrected. And none of us wants the corrections when we get them. So a master teacher must use a balance of encouragement, which is the **carrot**, and criticism, which is the **stick**. It's like driving a car, or more like a mule *[laughter]*. If they seem discouraged, you correct them with kindness and encouragement: "You did that really well. Now this time, do it like this." And sometimes though if the student is too proud, then you should use the stick and criticize them, even when they're doing it right. Sometimes it's not a question of correction—they're doing it pretty well, but they could go beyond that. So the carrot and stick are important for both correction and driving further. So if you're keeping score, there are four here.

I forgot one back at **stainless steel**—you can see your reflection in stainless steel. A great teacher must inspire and must encourage integrity among the students. A school soon falls apart if the teacher doesn't have integrity, and it is important for a student to have it as well. For example, a student who lies to a teacher is thwarting the process of correction and teaching, and it soon breaks down.

What's next? **A gas pedal, a general with the orders.** I try to learn new things often, to keep my brain from calcifying more, and I've noticed that if the teacher is going too fast you get discouraged, and if the teacher is going too slow you get bored. In either case you don't learn well. I think a great teacher has to be very sensitive to the speed a student can handle and try to use the **gas pedal** correctly.

General means that I think a teacher should have an aura of authority. They should come into the class and the students should shush down. There should be a quiet descending in the room when they enter, and there should be a sense of decorum. There should be a sense of respect for this teacher, no matter what subject it is. I think a teacher should try to encourage this atmosphere of respect for the teacher and for what's being taught. Students shouldn't interrupt the teacher frequently or sidetrack the class. The teacher should be in control of the class.

With the orders means, as a student even now of many teachers, I know how frustrating it is if the teacher won't tell you clearly what they want from you. You, as a student, very much want to please your teacher but sometimes they don't tell you what's required. You don't know what to do before the next class. You don't know what they expect from you. It should be very clear. A teacher should be carrying the papers with the orders, and they should give them to you.

Next. **A pillow.** As a student even now learning new things, I think the first few minutes or hours or days with a new teacher are very frightening. You're nervous, you're not sure if they're going to smack you on the head, or you're not very good at what they are teaching yet, and you feel some kind of lack of confidence. Often you're in a new building, there are other students there, and everything is strange and new and a little frightening or threatening even. I think a good teacher must have the ability to make you comfortable as you first enter. They should take time and pay attention to make sure you enter happily and smoothly. There'll be time later to smack them.

An ant with winter coming. We sat on the porch one day on the yurt and the red ants, whom I much admire, were in a long line. They were marching somewhere beyond the fence of the yurt, where we rarely go. In one direction all the ants were walking swiftly. Each one was carrying a tiny grain of seed, or things that looked like eggs, but we were afraid to make them drop one to check. In the other direction coming back were these poor fellows dragging their feet and obviously totally exhausted. And they would bump into each other and their antenna would meet, and I think they said, "Oh, it's a long way."

I followed the path they had worn with their tiny little legs. They had worn a four-inch path for hundreds of yards to their winter home, and they were carrying every single piece of tiny grain for winter. Much better than we, they had prepared for winter. I think a great teacher must enter the class completely prepared. I have met teachers who considered it a point of pride not to prepare. "I know *Madhyamika* hands down; I don't even need to look at the book before the class."

I don't think it's good. I think that when you start to teach your own students you must come into the class prepared. You should spend days, hours getting ready, making sure you have a plan.

Branching tunnels ready. This means that if you try to catch the mole who lives under my porch you never will, because he has three or four escape tunnels. So when you surprise him at the opening of one, he's already gone out the other way. I think a good teacher, when they enter a class with a plan, should be ready to change it on the spot.

Once I was invited to Kentucky to teach. I'd never been there. I said, "What do you want me to teach?" They said, "*Vinaya.*" That's monks' and nuns' discipline.

I said, "Do you know what *vinaya* is?" They said, "No, but it sounds good."

When I got there, it was four or five sort of strange people in an elementary school cafeteria. Venerable Chudrun-hla, holy Tessie, came along with some other people. We passed out *vinaya* teaching sheets and after two sentences, I switched to lamrim. And Venerable Tessie came to me afterwards, and said, "I saw you do that." You have to be ready to switch if the circumstances change. I think a good teacher has to be ready to switch to another tunnel.

A chameleon on the same old rock. Same old rock means consistency. A teacher's presentation should be consistent in two ways. You can count two here: on the rock. Internally what they teach has to be free of contradiction. They shouldn't say, "This is true," at one point and then teach something else which contradicts it a few minutes later. Internally what they teach has to be free of contradiction. The path they show you must be consistent. And then over time, over weeks and months and years, they shouldn't keep switching tracks to other things that contradict what they taught before. *Tartuk tekpa chikpa.* In the end all paths lead to the same goal. As they teach, they should teach the foundation first, and then move on to the higher levels. There should be a change of levels, but never a contradiction of what came before.

Now we get to the **chameleon**.

"So, are you saying great teachers never sound like they contradict themselves?"

Those of you who studied with the great holy master, the unsurpassable Geshe Thubten Rinchen in Sera Mey, those who had that fortune, know he taught us about how Lord Buddha contradicted himself in four great cycles of teaching. In four, or is it three? *[Laughter.]* As he moved up through the levels of teaching—especially teaching emptiness—he contradicted, or seemed to contradict, himself. And in the end, the great students realized it was all one smooth path.

A great teacher, I think, shouldn't be afraid to appear to contradict themselves if they think it would help the student. In the monastery, we often see a great old geshe stand up during the examination of a new geshe and propose something which is ridiculous, just to see if the baby geshe can defeat it. It's not that they really believe it. They are trying to help the student move higher. I think a great teacher has to have the internal strength to throw contradictions to their students, and be called a fool or crazy or contradictory, and watch the student's mind grow because of the contradiction.

Lawn of grass. I was thinking about holy Jerry Dixon's lawn, wondering how he could grow it. And it occurred to me that lawns have equanimity; they treat everyone the same. The lawn doesn't get bumpier for some people and smoother for others. A good lawn treats everybody's feet the same, and I think a great teacher treats all of their students the same. They don't favor one student, or two or three, over another. They want every student to succeed equally and they give their heart to each student equally.

Does it mean that they reveal the same teachings to each student? No. Some students are ready for a *sous sus,* some can do *port de bras,* some can't even stand in first position yet. Yet. It would be wrong to teach a beginner a move in dance that would hurt them. But they have equal concern for each student, equal love for each student, equal hope for their success.

Old temple gong. The process of correcting a student is very traumatic. You may think just for the student, but no, it's equally hard for the teacher. They have to pretend that they're not having a trauma when they hit you on the head. But when they go home, they feel sad that they had to be tough.

It's hard to be tough; everyone wants other people to like them. When a student needs to be corrected forcefully, and you do it, you go home feeling bad. As you correct them, you have to pretend that it was necessary, and I'm the master and you deserve it. But when you get home, you feel your heart aches.

And there are waves of emotion coming back from the student, sometimes even hatred. But this is what makes the music. The teacher has to be like a gong, and the student will beat them—emotionally, sometimes. The teacher has to take it and realize that this is what makes the beauty of the music. The teacher should be like a gong. There are big gongs, four or five feet across, at the top of the great monasteries of Tibet, and I was thinking of them.

Old means this process may go on for many years. It's not like you have one incident of harsh correction of a student and then everything's smooth after that. If harsh correction is necessary once, it's probably going to be necessary many times. So a great teacher, like an old gong, has to have perseverance and patience over a long period of time. The student, if they don't give up, will resist the master and resist correction, as we all do—as the master did with his master, or her master. A teacher has to have patience and great endurance and perseverance for the long run.

Pruning shears for a fresh sapling. On rare occasions it happens that a teacher, a master, realizes that a certain student cannot grow in their school. There's some kind of problem, they don't fit the place or the master. In business, in a large corporation, we saw a phenomenon where an employee who didn't really want to be there anymore didn't have the courage to leave and be without a job, but they hated the job. And so slowly they would start to disrupt the work. They were asking subconsciously to be fired, but they didn't have the courage to leave. They didn't even know themselves that they wanted to leave. And it happens in a school: a student doesn't fit; they're not growing.

I remember the first time it happened with me, and I went to my holiest teacher *[crying]* and I said, "I don't know what to do." My teacher said, "Cut them." I said, "I can't bear it."

31

And they said, "Sometimes you have to prune the tree so the other parts of the tree can grow properly."

So a teacher must have the courage and strength to cut a student who needs to go somewhere else. And then like a fresh cutting from a tree, I think a great teacher must try to find the person a new home. "I know a lama across town; maybe that's better for you. I talked to the lama. They think you might fit in." And then happily try to help them get a new start.

Mt. Meru and a rubber ball. What do Mt. Meru and a rubber ball have in common? In the Buddhist view of the universe, Mt. Meru is the central core of the entire world. It never moves. The whole universe moves around it. It's unshakable. Oftentimes in a school, and oftentimes in a relationship with a student, disasters occur. The school burns down, you lose the rent, or your greatest sponsor bails out suddenly. Suddenly you realize the whole place is bankrupt. The government passes a law against your religion. Things like this happen. A great teacher, a real master should be unshaken. The students rush in and say, "What will we do?"

And they say, "No problem. We'll figure it out."

They have to project, even if they don't feel, great confidence—unshakable confidence. "Oh this is lucky, now we can really grow."

Rubber ball means they should bounce right back. The next morning they have a plan for a new space, they have new ideas for how to support everything, they have found a way, and they just recover. If you hope to teach people important things, the more important it is, the greater the obstacles, and you have to get used to it. You can't be a wimp and collapse every time something bad happens. You won't be a good teacher.

A teacher of learning and teaching. I think one of the first things a great teacher must do with a new student is teach them how to be a student, because it's not easy to be a good student. No matter what you're learning the first thing to tell them is, "Look, you came here to learn something, you asked me to teach you, so I think it would be good if you do what I ask you to do. If I say move your left arm to the left, you should move your left arm to the left. Don't stare at me and say, 'I wanted to move my right arm.'"

If a student can't learn how to be a student and follow instructions, even from the first day, then it will surely fail; they will never learn anything. I'm sure you've been to schools, karate, or dance, or physics, and you've seen the great students. They are the ones who would stand at the edge of the rooftop, and the teacher says, "Jump," and they jump. They don't ask a question, they don't look back; they don't stare at the teacher. They just jump.

In every school there are two or three people like that. They are obviously budding masters. They're obviously going to be the next master. You can feel it. There's an excitement when you see them interact with the teacher. It's like a rudder and a boat. The teacher turns the rudder and the boat turns immediately. The boat doesn't ask the rudder, "Why did we go that way?" It's automatic. It's a great beauty to see, because you know that a person who can truly respond immediately without question to a master's instructions will surely become a master themselves. And it's a teacher's responsibility to recognize this and teach the student how to be a student.

I think the other great requirement of a student is to review. In Tibet, it was a very strict rule that every time you took a teaching, in the next twenty-four hours you would look at it three times. Even if it's only a few minutes, you would pull that paper out of your pocket and you would look at it again, and think about what you learned. It was a rule. I think it's a beautiful rule. If you review it three times in every twenty-four hours after that teaching, you will soon learn that thing perfectly. That's how to be a student.

Secondly, even from the beginning, the teacher should teach the student how to teach. It was such an honor to sit in Khen Rinpoche, my holy Lama's, class, year after year. We soon learned what he was teaching, but after awhile it just became a pleasure to watch how he taught. And this is something you should do. You should teach the student how to teach.

Learning and teaching: an honor. A very fortunate group of us studied with holy, incredible lama Geshe Thubten Rinchen at the monastery in India. And at the end, he said one thing I'll always remember. He said, "You think you're the ones who are learning. It's not you, it's me."

I asked him, "How did you become the world's greatest philosopher? I've never seen anything like it."

He said, "I learned by teaching."

For thirty years he has taught, almost without a day off, I think about sixteen hours a day. He has three hundred students, and he gives each one his whole heart. *[Crying.]* He said, "This is how I learned; I taught." It's a great honor to be a teacher. I think a great teacher realizes that they are the ones who are learning. We are very lucky to be asked to teach, because we can learn.

What's the next one? **A builder glad to go to first grade.** Builders are obvious. I didn't have any place else to put it in the verses. A great teacher builds a school. They build an organization so that people can come and learn. It's only a single word, school, but it's a tremendous amount of work, grief, suffering, expense, time, sweat, and disappointments. But if you wish to help people, you must build a school.

Glad to go to first grade means the great teachers love to learn. We had the honor to be asked to go to CNN. They were making a documentary about the sweet, incredible, holy Dalai Lama, His Holiness, and they couldn't figure out what was happening in some of their footage. I watched the monitor, and they played some footage taken recently. His Holiness was offering a mandala on a plate with rice, and I explained what it is.

And they said, "What's it for? Who's the man in front of him?"

And I looked closer and I listened to the conversation. And it suddenly struck me, here the greatest Buddhist master, *[crying]* the greatest human on this planet, is begging another person for a lesson. And he's asked people to film it so that the whole world can see the greatest teacher asking to be taught by another. And it was even a master of another tradition. So I think a great master has the quality of being willing to humble himself before other teachers and learn something new. It's hard for a person who is already a Nobel Prize winner and has taught Dharma since they were five years old to hundreds of thousands of people. But great masters are never finished learning and are always willing to go back to first grade.

What's the next one? Oh, **even in their own school.** Oftentimes a student will come up with a bright idea. Usually they are dumb *[laughter from students on* *stage*], but you and I know oftentimes there is a jewel. Someone comes up with a truly great idea: a change in the school, a different way of teaching, or even a different thing to teach. Maybe even an unexpected, new, beautiful insight into the subject.

A teacher should be happy and proud. They shouldn't react with some kind of pride. They should immediately, even in their own school, say, "That's beautiful. We should do it like that." It takes a lot of inner strength to admit those things and to see the beauty that a student can produce.

What's next? **Proud poppa.** A great teacher, when the student does something great, should be happy and proud. I sometimes sense in lesser teachers a sort of defensiveness, a fear that they are losing their grip on the student as it becomes apparent that the student is growing even beyond the teacher. I think a teacher should be proud to sit in the background as their student plays that piece even better than they ever did, and be completely pleased and proud that they have helped this person become something great.

What's next? **A push from the nest.** There can arise a sort of unhealthy co-dependent relationship between teachers and students. Sometimes the subject gets lost, and the student comes to cling to the teacher, and the teacher comes to cling to the student. They forget that the goal was to create a new master. I think a great teacher is hoping for the day that they can push the new bird from the nest, and they fly off with beautiful grace. I think every great teacher is happy to see the day when their production, their baby, flies into the sky on their own, and maybe starts a new school, and starts to teach their own students. And the teacher should anticipate and pray for the day they can push them out of the nest to help more people.

Next. **Genghis Khen and lieutenants.** You have to appreciate what the Mongols were, especially those of you who were in Mongolia, which is now impoverished, and their future is very uncertain. Now they could be crushed any moment, but in the twelve hundreds Genghis Khan had an empire. In the north, in Russia, they took Moscow. To the east, in one day, four hundred thousand Austrian troops were slain outside of Vienna. To the south, they covered the Middle East—Persia, Afghanistan, India. To the southeast, they went as far as Vietnam. To the northeast, as far as Korea and Beijing.

How did one man with just horses and sticks defeat an area that took three years on horseback to cover from east to west? It took three years to send an instruction to the front lines.

He had a special skill. He would take a trusted lieutenant, often a relation, and say, "You conduct this campaign. I won't say anything. I will stand behind you at the meetings and I will give my suggestions to you privately later on, but you're on your own."

And so even before he died, even while he was still strong and young, he had the foresight to build other people as lieutenants to take over everything. And they did, even to his grandsons. So I think a great teacher builds great teachers below them, and then has the foresight to release the school to those teachers, so that the school is strong and healthy for a long time. Only by reaching beyond themselves can a teacher truly create something that will help many people, and by creating qualified people underneath them to take care of new students.

What's next? **A maker and passer of the torch.** This is a similar idea. I think it's a great teacher's responsibility to record what they know in any kind of medium. It could be books, it could video, it could be computers, it could be human hearts, but they take the time and trouble and foresight to make a system, to create a body of material that will last beyond them. This is the torch. They take care after they have organized this body of material to transmit it fully, carefully, to their best students. And then they pass it.

Oftentimes a lesser teacher grasps on to the power of teaching too long. They are getting old and they haven't trained new students, and then the knowledge dies with them. The school fairly quickly falls apart. There's no one who has been trained. There's no one who has been blessed by the master, "This is the next carrier of the torch. These three, four, or ten people are now your teachers. I will be here, I will lend a hand, and I will give my advice from time to time, but these people are now in charge." And bless them, and grant them the torch. That way the torch goes on for many generations.

I don't remember, but I think we're on the hundred and fiftieth or something holder of the throne of Je Tsongkapa, the teacher of the first Dalai Lama. We have qualified lamas because of this making of the torch, which the holy incomparable master Je Tsongkapa made in his works and his monasteries that he built. Then he passed it on, and that is why we have it today, because it became a tradition to pass it on, and not try to own it, or grasp to it until you die.

Please be patient, I know it's going to get colder, and I know it's going long, but I think it's important to be said once. You should take these papers home and keep them with you for years. Pull them out from time to time and look at them and say, "How do I match up? How am I doing against these ninety-one or so qualities? Do I have them yet?"

What was the next one? **A spider in a big web.** I think a great teacher should have access to resources. Throughout their life, they should be building resources. They should have great teachers who they have gone to that they can turn other people on to. They should know where the great books are. They should know the great pieces of music and should have collected the scores. They should know where to find the best dorjes and bells. They should build a huge network of resources for their students in anticipation.

There's a holy, secret, quiet lama, Sharpa Rinpoche, posing as a normal layman, and he was kind enough to give me some of my first lessons in India. *[Cries.]* And one day a guy came and said, "I am selling [copies of] *Lamrim Chenmo,* do you want one?" It was this huge beautiful manuscript.

And I said, "No, I can't read it. I'll never be able to read it."

Sharpa Rinpoche said, "Buy it!" And I did.

You should get these things ready, even years beforehand. Be ready with everything you need to serve your students. Don't let a Dharma teaching pass you without recording it or making notes. Make it ready for the next generation. Prepare yourself.

What's next? **Peer revelry.** Some people say, "You made a boo-boo; it's peer rivalry." I thought peer revelry is better.

You often see lesser masters who are so sickly jealous of each other that it's sad. Even a new student can see it. They say, "Don't go to the guy across the street, that yoga school is bad."

"Why?"

"They don't turn their head the way we do."

And you say, "Doesn't seem like such a big thing to me."

And then slowly you realize it's just a matter of professional jealousy, and it's very sad for a new student. I think great masters don't have this problem. They revel in the accomplishments of other masters. They don't get jealous. They hear that a new book has come out by another master. They jump, they read it; they send a note: "That's such a beautiful thing you've done. It's wonderful." And then lesser masters are jealous. They find the comma missing on page 48, and send a note.

So as you approach your teacherhood, take special care for this kind of pride. It's very evil; we all have it. I have a bad case of it. You have to try to rejoice at the accomplishments of everyone. We are supposedly working for the happiness of every living being, and then we get jealous and wish that this person hadn't done something beautiful.

What's next? **A free referral service.** I think you often see teachers getting possessive of students. "I have three hundred and sixty four; you only have three hundred and fifteen. I'm a better person. I'm a better teacher."

Rarely will you find a master who will sit down and say, "Look, there's another teacher a few doors down who really knows how to play Chopin much better than I do, to be honest. I want you to go for a few weeks and learn what they know. You're welcome to come back. I love you as my student. I feel proud to have you as my student. But I also see that you could grow even more if you would go and learn this thing from someone else. And then come back; maybe you can teach me."

This is a healthy free referral service. No strings attached. "You go and you grow with this new teacher. And I wish you the best. And, then come back when you're done, and we'll keep going."

What's next? **A piggy bank, a teddy bear and a bureaucrat.** I've mentioned this many times, but it's so wonderful. I don't mean to bore you, or freeze you, to mention it again. In Sera Monastery, the teachers don't get a penny. It's always been like that. They give their lives. Geshe Thubten Rinchen has tuberculosis from working too hard for free. Gyalrong Khensur Rinpoche, the *vinaya* master who taught you, has tuberculosis from working his whole life for free, and not having enough food. Not only that, but when they accept a student in Sera they accept responsibility for all their financial needs.

You don't pay to be student at Sera. The teacher pays to have an idiot come in and abuse them for twenty years. And they do it. So I think when a great teacher has a close student, and the student needs something, they take care of it. And I encourage all of you, and me too, to live like that. Such a holy way. They don't charge you; they pay for you. Dharma should always be free.

There are cases in other fields where a teacher must charge to live to go on and teach. I'm not talking about that. That's a proper charge. It should be reasonable. There should be exceptions for students who can't pay. But in our field, in learning how to serve others—there's no price for this.

Khen Rinpoche and I were speaking one day and wondering how people could charge for something that doesn't have a price. What are you going to pay someone for eternal happiness? So a great teacher should help their students with their material needs when the time comes.

Teddy bear means a great teacher should also help a student in times of emotional need. I can remember when a student's parent died and they would come to their holy Lama and cried literally on his shoulder, and he would be there for them. Even as a teacher of music or architecture, when you're a master and you have this relationship with the student, you should be there for them when they need you.

But I should also say that I don't think it's appropriate, and it doesn't work, to try to fulfill all the emotional needs of a student. You can't. A master can't teach the subject that they are teaching and be the psychiatrist and mother and father of all their students. There's no possible time, and it's not healthy, I think. So in times of need, I think a great teacher should be there as a comfort, but not a sort of dependency, which is not healthy for either, and not healthy for the school.

What's next? Oh, **bureaucrat.**

Frankly, if you decide to teach people, and you must, you will have to become a junior bureaucrat. How to get that tax exemption, how to get the rent lease straightened out, how to get the books running smoothly, so the IRS doesn't lock you all up. This is something that you are going to have to face as a teacher. Many people avoid it, and they get in trouble.

You have to rent or find a place where the school can happen. You have to find the money and sponsors for the needs of the students. You have to drag a piano upstairs yourself. This is the job of the teacher. It's an honor. It's a trouble.

Next, **golden magnet.**

Golden has two meanings. **Magnet** means that once you have matured to a certain point as a teacher, you realize that it is your responsibility to attract good students. Normally, it seems there might be danger of pride, and there is in advertising yourself. But if you're a true master, and you have tried to control your pride, you should not be afraid of publicity. You should use it wisely. You should travel and meet people, always looking for that special person who could become a master. And then quite without embarrassment, hook them.

Different people like different things. Some people get hooked with curry macaroni *[laughter]*. Some people need something else, maybe a certain kind of rock and roll music. Find out what they like, study what they like, and attract them. This is in the list of the six Buddhist perfections. There's a list of ten; it's one of the last four: *dui ngopo shi*—the four ways to attract high quality people.

So I think a great master is like a magnet. They go out in the world consciously, proactively, looking for great material. That's half the golden part. They're looking for the kind of intelligence, brightness, emotional depth—all the great qualities of a student—and they are actively trying to attract great material, like a gymnastics coach.

The other part of golden means that as a teacher you have to be attractive to the people you wish to find. It may involve taking on different guises. Sometimes you may have to look like a businessman. Sometimes maybe like a monk. Maybe sometimes like a hippie. You should try to look and speak in a way which attracts the people you hope to teach. This is an ancient Buddhist method.

In the Diamond Cutter Sutra, *(whose translation was requested by a certain holy being—I hope it's been corrected)* the Buddha gets up before he teaches, and what does he do? He changes his robe and brushes his teeth, because a teacher should be attractive to the student. Even in 2500 BC, nobody wanted to study with a teacher who had bad breath. It's your responsibility as a teacher. If it involves eating in a certain way, or exercising in a certain way, or buying certain clothes that you don't even like, carrying yourself in a certain way, speaking in a colloquial way, you must be ready to do that, because the teaching is more important than what you like.

What's next? *It's getting cold—I hope he goes faster.* **Symphony conductor.** A great teacher, especially of a dharma school, should be able to handle the needs and demands of a large group of people. It's very hard. Holy Lama Zopa Rinpoche has mastered it. He serves thousands of people every day with grace and with great poise and with great compassion, even though these demands have ruined his body. *[Cries.]* And the symphony part means a teacher must struggle to encourage harmony among the students. It's typical, almost universal, that students rival with each other. They try to outdo each other.

There was a holy man who lived in the Middle East. He was having his last meal on this planet *[cries]* with his twelve holy disciples. He was about to be taken away to be spat upon and beaten and torn and nailed up. What were the disciples talking about?

"Which of us is greatest, Master? Which of us will be most famous?"

And he turned to them and says, "Some people serve the food; some people eat the food. I came to serve the food." *[Still crying.]* "The greatest of you will be the one who figures out that you should serve the others. The greatest of you twelve will be the one who is the lowest and serves the rest."

So if even in such circumstances there can be arguments going on among students, of course they are happening among us. A teacher must try to prevent this, with good humor and with patience. A great teacher will force the two students who dislike each other the most to work together. It's very hard. When you get home, you're drained and dismayed that two holy beings could be jealous like that in a holy place, but you have to try to get them to learn to respect and rejoice in each other's practices.

41

What's next? **An old pair of shoes. Old pair of shoes** has two meanings.

If anyone gets all ninety-one, I don't know…I'll loan you the caretakers for a day. In the diamond business, there's a lot of show. It's a business of smoke and mirrors. Nothing is real. These little rocks don't mean anything. When you go to a new city to buy diamonds, you always stay in the best hotel, and you rent the most expensive room. Why? Because the seller will believe you have enough money to pay for the diamonds you buy, even if you spent your last penny to pay for the hotel room. So I've eaten in the greatest hotels in the world. Unwillingly, I have stayed in the most expensive rooms in the world. I have never had service like this. It's unbelievable. You would love it. I'm not kidding and I'm not exaggerating. I've never been taken care of like this. Never. Nothing close.

What was the next one? Oh, **old shoes**. A great teacher should be like a pair of old shoes. I went to a place in India called Palitana. I was asked to go by the most incredible holy man, Dhiru Shah, a sweet holy man. We planned to walk up the holy mountain, before dawn, which is the custom, to be in the small, beautiful Jain temple as the sun rose. It's a custom to go without shoes. And I said, "OK."

Six hours later, when I got back down to the bottom, I went to my old shoes, and I kissed them. My feet were torn to ribbons. I said, "No one appreciates shoes. No one takes their shoes off at night and says, 'Thank you for protecting me all day from rocks and thorns.'"

Strangely, the farther you take a student, the less they thank you, normally. It's very rare that a student truly understands what they have received, and I think that a great teacher should live without expectation of thanks or gratitude. I think this is very important to understand or you'll be disappointed. You have to believe in what you're teaching so much that you may never hear thanks, and you will never worry about it.

The other part of old shoes is that they are dependable. A great teacher should have an aura of dependability and predictability. A student should feel, "This person will always be there for me." Physically, if it's possible, they should be in a steady location, traveling perhaps, but always coming back. People know if I go there, they'll be near. This is dependable; I can count on it. When they say they'll do something, they do it, and they'll always be there for you. That's another quality.

Next? **Old hat.** Old hat means if you have a chance to go to an older master teacher, this is something wonderful. They have experience teaching.

An older monk, holy Gendun Gyatso, came to me on a snowy day in New Jersey. He had been shoveling snow, and he had an intense pain in his chest. We rushed him to the hospital in the blizzard, and immediately he was surrounded by young interns and expensive machines and they were pushing things into his body. I called our old country doctor, and said, "Please come. It's a serious heart attack, they say."

He came in the snow. He was about 75, and he hobbled in. He was drunk as usual. He lifted up the shirt, and said, "Shingles," and he turned around and left.

And I ran after him, and said, "What's shingles?"

"It's a kind of chicken pox. It goes along your rib, and you feel like you've had a heart attack." And he turned again.

And I said, "Stop, what shall we do?"

And he said, "Nothing to do. It goes away."

The interns were so embarrassed. They gave him some aspirin and we went home.

This is experience. A great teacher has experience. "I've seen fifty students make that mistake. Don't do that, okay? I've been through it. Don't try to convince me that you should do it that way. I've seen it over and over and over." Ironically, no one listens anyway. But experience is very precious. That's the old hat.

I think at this point, we should take a break. Are we halfway? Three-quarters. Three-quarters is good. Let's take a break. I hope you've brought something warm to drink. Share it with the other people here. This is a custom at the winter debates. We all stay "sempe damcha" all night long. We stay for debates, to watch the great teams from the monasteries fight it out. Sera Mey always wins. [Laughter.] Sera Jey always disgraces themselves [more laughter], as far as I can tell.

And we all share a big "tukpa", a big oatmeal together. The little monks run in with it, and the first guy spills it on someone's head. It's like a comedy. The second guy runs in and slips on the first guy's oatmeal, and soon everyone is eating it and covered. But it's warm. So share something with each other and bundle up, and we'll go on after that.

Don't be shy. In the winter debates, we just sit and chomp. So feel free, and enjoy. We'll keep going.

What's next? **An active player.** When you learn dance or music or art, it's so much more fun when the teacher is still doing what they're teaching. Sometimes it's not possible, due to their age or other circumstances. But if it's possible I think it's good to find a teacher who's actually doing what they're teaching.

"Come tonight to the concert hall. You can hear me play that song."

"Come to the basketball game tonight. Watch me wipe out Magic Johnson." *[Laughter.]*

If you have a teacher who is still active, it's more precious; one who is still doing what they teach.

By their own game plan means one of the four great qualities of a teacher in the ten perfections. They should be doing things the way they teach them. It's very discouraging to have a teacher who describes to you the benefits of a daily book, or of meditation, or retreat, or kindness to others, who's obviously not doing it themselves. So perhaps this should have been one of the first qualities, I think. It's so much more powerful when you can see that the teacher is doing as they preach, and it's so discouraging when you see that they are not doing it as they preach at all. This is following the game plan.

What's next? A kid? *(Laughter.)* **A kid single-pointed on a double scooped cone.** It's too cold for that. Let's say double marshmallows on a campfire. *(Laughter.)* The **kid** part means energy. A teacher, I think, needs to have energy. They can be eighty years old and still have energy. Energy means they have this kind of childlike love and energy for the subject, and they can go all night long. Lama Zopa Rinpoche, holy being, has energy. His Holiness has energy. I have seen both lamas very ill and still teaching with total energy. A teacher needs energy. It also means you have to take care of yourself. If you're going to teach, you'll need tons of energy. It's a process of giving energy, and you have to take good care of

44

yourself. Know when to sleep. Know how to eat. Know when to say "no."

Single-pointed means there's a quality of intensity, which is different from energy. Energy means the ability to stay up all night; intensity means when they see that subject, they jump on it like a hungry dog on a steak. They dig in; they gobble it down. You should see holy Lama Geshe Thubten Rinchen with a new book on something like difficult *Drange* philosophy. The light's on all night. He comes out in the morning with blurry eyes. "That was great!" *[Laughter.]* You have to have intensity that a child would have for an ice cream cone on a warmer day.

Double scooped cone means some people have energy and intensity for their subject of which they are a master, but not for teaching. Some people have energy and intensity for teaching, but not for learning what they're trying to teach. I think a great master and teacher should have this energy and intensity and love and joy for what they do, and for passing it on, equally.

Next is **a gem carver.** Often in the diamond business, people will walk in with a stone, and say, "What's this thing?" I remember a man who walked in with a yellow stone. He said, "I risked my life to bring this out of Tibet." And I said, "It's a piece of quartz."

There are special instruments we use, refractometers, special chemicals, specific gravity liquids, many different tools to find out what the stone is. But in Gemology school, when they taught us about jade, it was so interesting. They said, "When someone comes with a large carving of jade, just step back and look at the quality of the carving, and you can find out if it's jade or nephrite or some other inexpensive stone. No Chinese emperor with a huge piece of jade is going to give it to an amateur to carve. If the quality of the carving is exquisite, it's probably jade."

This means that great masters go for the greatest subject. The greatest teachers are attracted to the greatest subjects. Holy Lama Geshe Thubten Rinchen is the undeniable master of Sera Mey of *Madhyamika* (Middle Way), *Prajnaparamita* (Perfection of Wisdom), *Pramana* (Logic and Perceptual Theory), *Drange* (how to interpret difficult parts of Buddha's teaching). He doesn't teach the easier subjects. The great teachers are attracted to the great subjects.

In our case please remember that the greatest subject is serving others, higher than those other subjects. You want to try to find a teacher who has mastered the greatest subjects. Holy Lama Zopa Rinpoche can't stop talking about compassion. Holy Lama Khen Rinpoche can't stop teaching emptiness and the higher teachings. The great ones are attracted to the great subjects. So try to find a teacher who has the courage to bite off the most difficult highest subjects.

What's next? **A new edition of an old book.** I think a great teacher, in their early years, must first master the entire tradition of the generations who came before them. I urge each of you not to be lazy about this. Don't become one of those shallow teachers who doesn't really know the depth and breadth of their tradition. You have been gifted by Holy Lama Khen Rinpoche and others with the entire depth of a great ocean of wisdom. Don't ignore it. Learn the whole thing.

Master the tradition first. But then, when it comes time to present what you've learned to normal people, then make it a new edition. Don't change the wisdom, there's no need, but present it according to modern times. This is one of the greatest teachings of *vinaya*. The last few lines of the Vinaya Sutra are, "And these rules must be adjusted to the times in which you live, with great wisdom, and carefully." And so I think a great master must master the tradition and then have the wisdom to present it in a way which is relevant and accessible to their times.

What's next? **Triple evolution.** This is a similar idea. Young masters delight in virtuosity. Young piano masters want to see how much complicated music they can play quickly. Young dancers of ballet want to see how many jumps they can do in three minutes, how many turns. This is the concern of a younger master, and it's a good thing.

A middle-aged master, I think, graduates to the accessible. They don't want to overwhelm the audience. They want the audience to be able to participate. They want what they know to be accessible to anyone. They're not concerned with making fifteen jumps quickly. They want something which everyone can appreciate during the entire performance, and go home happy. A middle aged dharma master wants the people that they teach not to become a master of many complicated things, but to learn to take that complicated knowledge and transmit it in a clear and accessible way to others.

In the final evolution of a master, I think they begin to understand the eternal and the classical. Even beyond the accessible, they want to achieve simplicity and perfection in a few words: things that are timeless, a short teaching which will benefit their listeners for many years. I think His Holiness the Dalai Lama has this quality. He can give a half-hour teaching and touch upon the eternal truths in an accessible way, because he's a virtuoso in thousands of texts. I think Jesus would have similar skill.

Next? **Trail blazer and lion.** If you truly master a body of wisdom, if you digest an entire tradition, even in piano or dance or yoga or anything, you naturally come to the edge of the frontier. And then you naturally forge ahead to uncharted territory. You become an innovator. In Tibetan philosophy, this is called *shingta sulje.* It means, "the guy who invented the first cart." You can think of him as Henry Ford. It means someone who has vision, someone who has mastered the tradition, and then takes it one step forward. They are rare. There are only three *shingta sulje* normally recognized: Master Asanga from 300 AD, Master Nagarjuna from 200 AD, and Je Tsongkapa. They brought into this world a new vision based on the old tradition, an extension, a further awakening of the ancient knowledge in a new direction.

I think every great master does this in their own way, and they take us further. Not to new wisdom: the emptiness taught by the innovator Master Nagarjuna, the compassion taught by the great innovator Master Asanga, the marriage of karma and emptiness and compassion by Je Tsongkapa, cannot be improved upon or rivaled. But great masters can take us in new directions of appreciating these great truths in a new way. In so doing, they stick their head up above the crowd, which is always dangerous. Someone will not like it.

The great Master Dharmakirti said, *"kyewo pelcher pel la chak shing sherab tsel mepe na lekshe nam, dundu mi nyer konar ma se trakdok drima dag gi dang war yang."*

He was defending his great master, Dignaga, both great logicians. He was saying, "The majority of people in the world don't even care about wisdom. They are attached to hamburgers and milkshakes. They can't appreciate what they hear. And those few who do understand are stricken by the great disease of jealousy."

And so often a person who goes beyond, like Galileo, Einstein, and Jesus, end up being hurt by those who don't understand what they have seen. They have a vision to take us beyond what we were before, and it's often dangerous for that person. They have to be a lion. They have to have the courage to stand out and to say,

47

"This is a new direction. I know you're not used to it, but this will take us further, and this will get us to our goal more quickly. This is a brave new world. This is a new thing."

And they have to have the knowledge and strength and the courage to defend the new direction against lesser and often well-intentioned thinkers. They have to be a lion, not in a bitter, competitive, or destructive way, but in a holy way, to explain what vision they've had

What's next? **A golden retriever and a koala bear.** *[Laughs.]* What do a golden retriever and a koala bear have in common? As the lion defends the new ideas, great masters also develop a kind of contentment, a kind of confidence in their knowledge and in their strength. A great powerful master doesn't find it necessary to crush smaller people, to fight them or beat them. They are like a golden retriever, one of largest of all dogs, and one of the most gentle, rarely showing their true power, never being angry. So I think a great master, when the time is right, should be a lion. Against serious, well-thought, worthy criticism, they should respond with a lion's roar. In Tibetan, it's called, *Sengge ngaro.*

But then when lesser criticism comes, or criticism which is not well thought out, or even when a student is acting up, they shouldn't show the full extent of their power. They should be like, I imagine, holy Lama Jerry Dixon.

(Someone might say), "Jerry, you're an idiot, you don't know how to build anything. You can't make a real estate deal." And I can see him leaning back in his chair, and saying, "You know, you might have a point there." *[Laughter.]* You don't have to show your strength. Be like a koala bear.

I had a chance to watch a series on lessons given by one of the greatest American masters of an ancient Indian yoga tradition, and it suddenly struck me that he hadn't shown what he could do once, in many hours. I had seen photographs of unbelievable power, strength, grace, and in real life, in front of students, he didn't reveal all that he knew once. He didn't even come close to showing off. I think it's a quality of a great master that they take what they are great at, and they put it in their little koala bear pouch. When it's time, they use it for good things, and when it's not time, they don't show it off.

Je Tsongkapa, the teacher of the first Dalai Lama and the founder of our lineage, was the greatest Sanskrit scholar of Tibet's history. He was also the greatest medical doctor in Tibet's history. No one knows. He didn't show it off. He kept it secret. It's obvious, and it was recorded in his biographies by his close students. If you know, and you look carefully among his writings, you can see it, but he didn't tell anyone. A great teacher should be like a koala bear.

What's next? **Gold to cut or file or melt.** Tibet had a currency, called *shos*, but in earlier societies, in the lack of a currency expensive things were traded for gold. "You give me a lump of gold, and I'll give you these three yaks." But in the absence of a Department of Commerce, you would have to check that gold. It might be a little covering on a piece of lead. One of the great skills in the ancient world was always to file a piece of gold or cut it with some shears, or to melt it, to tell if it was real gold.

This image was used by Lord Buddha in many teachings when he was begging his students to ask him difficult questions. "Don't ever take what I say, just because you like me. Never accept what the Buddha said just out of respect. Critique it, rip it apart, analyze it, and examine it. I'd love it, because a person who does that will sooner or later understand truth, and a person who just accepts anything I say will accept any other foolish thing that someone else says tomorrow."

So a great teacher, I think, welcomes difficult questions. They welcome a student to debate with them, and they're not at all afraid of debating and defending their understanding in the world, in front of other people. Not in an unpleasant, unfriendly way, but in the way that two great wise men question each other, like Socrates. And not in a defensive way, and not in a disruptive way. A student must pick the proper time in a respectful way to ask their difficult question, and a teacher will be very happy. A true master will rejoice that a student is thinking about these things.

What's next? **A scientist and a detective.**

I'm sorry it's cold. The object tonight is to suffer a little, which is a custom to show that you're serious. In the monastery, they sometimes require us to sit out in the rain for a few hours in the debate ground, or in the cold, and the debate master, who is the only one who can release us, goes home for a warm cup of tea. It's to strengthen us, and it's good—sometimes.

49

I think a great teacher should be like a scientist. The great scientists are the first ones to say, "I don't know." I saw a very moving scientific analysis of aging in National Geographic. It was very well done, with all of the information about how each part of the body collapses over the length of your life, and the last sentence that I remember was, "But to be honest, as scientists, we don't really know why people get old." I think a great teacher should be like a true scientist, and be willing to say when they don't know something. Quite openly, be willing to say, "It's a good question, and I haven't figured it out yet."

The next one is a detective. I can't imagine a true teacher who would stop at a question and say, "Oh yeah, that's a good question. I don't know." I think they would go home and dig through the ACIP database, or some scriptures, and try to figure it out by the next day, even if they stayed up all night. I think a great teacher goes home and crunches the problem until they figure it out, and then they come back to the student with wisdom.

What's next? **A word to the wise.** Old masters are often grumpy. They are often very set in their ways, but I think the greatest ones welcome correction. And I think the lesser ones when they are corrected, they try to turn it away or they try to ignore it. They even might say, "No, that's wrong," when they know it's right. I think a real master accepts correction quickly and gracefully, and then they change. It's an important quality in a teacher. A student is expected to respond to correction and instructions, and then if the teacher can't respond gracefully and meaningfully to a good correction, even from a student, I think it becomes apparent they're not such a master.

A ballerina.
We're almost done—have hope.
I think a great teacher should have a quality which is hard to find a word for, but it's like poise. It's the poise of a great ballerina on a stage—it's grace. When you see His Holiness the Dalai Lama approaching the stage, you see this kind of noble grace, or poise. And then as he approaches and steps up to the lectern, you can feel this kind of natural grace and poise in front of people. I think a great teacher, who really knows what they're teaching, who's a true old master, develops this kind of aura around them of poise.

What's next? **One or two gathered or in the arena.** I used to be an altar boy in a holy church not too far from here. There were three services: one at 7:30, one at 9:15, and one at 11:00 on Sunday mornings. The diehards came to the 7:30, the family people came to the 9:15 and the 11:00 service was for lazy people who couldn't get up.

This was a large church with thousands of people. One morning I was with the great holy minister, Father Urbano, who has left this world *[crying]*. We dressed in the back, we put on our robes, and we brought out the holy wine and wafers, we lit the candles, and we waited for 7:15. We made our entrance to the altar, and in this church, which holds several thousand people, there wasn't a single person. And we looked up at the father. We were hoping we could go home. And he said, "Jesus said, 'when one or two are gathered together ....' We will hold the service."

It was perhaps the most beautiful ritual that I have ever been in, because it was held for the right reason. I think a great teacher doesn't care if there are three people listening or three thousand listening. They know what they are teaching is important, they know how precious a single human spark of life is, and they don't care about how many people are there. I urge you, as teachers, especially in the beginning, you're not going to have hundreds of people coming and admiring your teaching. You will be with one or two confused young Americans in a little room somewhere, and you will say, "There's this thing, lamrim." And you should feel pride and honor to turn the holy wheel of the dharma on this planet once again.

In the arena means you should try—I know it's hard for many people—to develop the ability to stand in front of many people and speak without being nervous. I used to stop, and when I grabbed the handle to the door of the room in which I was teaching and my hand was shaking, I would say to myself, "This is not for you. This is for the good of many beings."

You shouldn't be so proud as to worry about how you look or what people will say. That's where nervousness really comes from. You are giving a holy gift today. You should speak with great confidence and courage. Don't think about yourself. I think a teacher must learn this. I know it's hard at the beginning for many people. You have to see it as an obstacle to be removed. You have to force yourself to learn to speak in front of many people with confidence.

What's next? **A seal in a quiet sea.** *This is the last verse—rejoice. That warm bed is waiting, and dinner.* There are three qualities in this seal in a quiet sea. We used to surf, and my holy mother would come and watch from the cliffs, in K-forty-two, which means forty-two kilometers south of the border. One day I saw this flash in the water next to me. It was some kind of a creature, gray, fast, and I paddled as fast as I could to get out of the water. I got up on the cliff, and my mother was standing there, laughing. I said, "What kind of a mother, to laugh when a shark is about to eat her son?"

And she said, "Turn around and look," and there were these beautiful seals playing. They would follow you as you surfed away; they would follow inside the wave. So we went out and played with them. It was incredible. They have this capacity for joy and good humor. I think if you want to be a great teacher, like His Holiness the Dalai Lama, like holy Lama Khen Rinpoche, or Zopa Rinpoche, or Geshe Thubten Rinchen, holy being, you have to learn to laugh, especially when things go wrong in the class, or the microphone breaks, or something happens. You have to have good humor. You can't be grumpy and teach many people. It won't work.

The second meaning of the quiet sea is that you have to know how to relax. I think a great teacher of many people must know when it's time to settle back and relax. I'm afraid that many great masters have lost or never had the ability to relax. It's hard to have energy and intensity, and then also to know when to take it easy and relax. If a teacher has many students and a very demanding schedule, then at a certain point, the students will even be hurt if the teacher doesn't know how to relax.

Lastly, the meaning of a quiet sea is a kind of serenity. A true master, especially the older ones, develop a kind of serenity and softness about them, a kind of peace that comes from having done something good your whole life, and I think it's important to try to emulate this serenity. I was had the honor of working for a brief time on a treatise with the abbot of Tashi Lumpo monastery, the seat of the Panchen Lama. His name was Tharchin Supa; he has left this world [crying]. He was holy Lama Thubten Rinchen's tantric master.

I anxiously awaited the moment of our meeting. I entered his chambers. It was an empty mud room with a little straw pallet over in the corner, and there was a toothless old man with all these little puppies on his lap, and he was giving them love. I thought I had gone into the wrong room. The greatest tantric master in South India, the greatest logician, and he had this serenity. He laughed the whole time, and he said, "Thif if the meaning of thif verfe. It'f unbelievable." [Laughter.] He didn't even have the pride to put in his teeth. He knew how to relax with the

52

puppies, and he had grace and serenity. We should try to be like that. No pride at all. And he would be bouncing up and down on the bed out of excitement when we got to a hard part.

This is the last one. **A match made in heaven.**

To put it briefly, you want to find the perfect teacher for you, the perfect match. You want someone who's just right for you, almost as if some higher power had arranged this marriage. You want that; you yearn for that. Deep in your heart, you want to find the perfect teacher. Tomorrow, I'd like to speak about how to find them.

In closing, I'd like to ask you to look at the next page—I hope it's there. It looks like an empty chart. As I gave this talk, and as we went over all ninety-something qualities of a truly great teacher, I'm sure you were thinking of a teacher. It might have been myself in some cases. Perhaps it was many other people who have taught you, but in your mind, deep in your heart, as we went through this list, you were comparing your teachers and yourselves against it. And I believe that, as we got to different qualities, you said, "Oh yes, my teacher has that 100%. I'm so lucky."

And then I'm equally sure that when we reached some other qualities, you said, "I'm sad, deep in my heart, to say I don't see that in my teacher. I wish I did."

It's politically correct in Buddhism to say the guru is perfect. You're not supposed to say my lama has this flaw, perhaps even a serious flaw. You're supposed to say and think, "Oh, my lama is perfect."

I want to encourage you to take home this list, the blank one. There's a column that says, "I do see," and there's a column that says, "I don't see." I really want you before tomorrow's teaching, maybe tomorrow morning as you're sleeping off your new cold—put a few pillows under your head; your nose won't run so much—and look at that list. Look at the qualities and fill it in: top five on each side. "These five qualities my teacher truly has, and I rejoice. It's a blessing." And then on the other side, "I don't see that my teacher has these qualities."

You won't see this kind of approach in a teaching very often. We aren't supposed to admit that we see a flaw, and maybe even a serious flaw, in our teacher. I give you special permission tonight to be completely honest with whatever is deep in your heart. Make this list. Be very brutally honest with your deepest feelings. "I really don't think that that teacher I have, or had, had this quality. They were not a golden retriever, to be honest, or they didn't look like it to me."

It's okay to say, "It didn't look like," but be honest when you fill in this list. The T.D.F.O. is a big secret. You don't get to find out unless you make yourself come back tomorrow. But bring the list tomorrow. You don't have to show it to anyone; I'll be embarrassed. But bring the list; we'll need it tomorrow.

That's all.

T.	D.	F.	O.

Third Day:

Saturday, March 10, 2001

What makes the Teacher perfect?

III.

Both good and bad are imprints;
Nothing was ever anything else.
Learn to maintain the good ones
And learn to rip out the bad.

Pushed into this life
On the dying gasp
Of a great saint;
Living off another's credit.

Born on the down escalator
Turn and double-time up;
Very few get ahead,
Very few even notice.

"Look the other way."
"Compromise; make the best of it."
"Struggle with them."

56

"Move on."
"You are bad. Just stop it."
"Find some good in it."
"It's a test."

No, take control
Of your destiny:
Make your teacher perfect.

Locate and cut the imprint, new or old,
By doing the opposite for others, unilaterally.
A transformation will come, or did,
Or another or more, or both.

Hard or soft,
Use emptiness and
The act of truth;
We have no other choice.

In an empty teacher
There need be no will;
Not an excuse for the corrupt—
Their reward is the hell they hoped for.

And so the process
Of making your perfect Teacher
Makes you perfect;
This itself is the teaching
The magic of empty teachers.

Oh please do come
And use your teacher so.

I thought not to do a real meditation, but just to be quiet for a few minutes.

Today is March 10ᵗʰ, and in 1959 in the capital of Tibet on this day, there were rumors that the occupying army might try to hurt His Holiness. And so tens of thousands of people from the city walked with bare hands to the Potala where His Holiness lived, and they blocked the whole place with their bodies. Then from hillsides nearby, the army from another country started to shell them [crying], and also they started to shell the place where His Holiness lived.

And so many unarmed people using their bodies stood between the cannons and the palace, and they tried to protect His Holiness. Many people died, and His Holiness was able to slip out in the confusion.

And so [sobs], and so, really we owe all that we have received as such a gift to the bravery of these people, six million prisoners in their own country. And so try to think a little bit of gratitude for them on the anniversary of their great sacrifice.

[Pause.]

OK. It's not too late to help the Tibetan people, and there are many fine projects to help them. I hope that all of us will keep trying to help them for many years.

There's a scene in the Bible. Jesus entered a small village, and a blind man heard it was him, and cried out, "Will you heal my eyes?"

And Jesus did a sTrange thing. He went to the man and took him by the hand, and he said, "Walk out of the village to a distance with me."

And so a few disciples came, and they walked far from the village. And he said, "Kneel down." And Jesus spat on his hands, rubbed his fingers on the man's eyes and said, "Open your eyes."

The man opened them, and Jesus said, "Can you see?"

And the man said, "I see sTrange things like trees, but moving."

Jesus said, "Those are people. But I think you need a little more."

And he rubbed his eyes more. And then the man opened them and saw everything perfectly. You can imagine how it felt. He said to Jesus, "I'll do anything. What can I do to repay you?"

And Jesus said, "Two things. First, don't go back to the village for awhile, until I am far gone. And secondly, don't tell anyone I did it."

And sometimes, when I wonder how everything could be so wonderful here, I think it's because almost every single person connected with this attempt has done their help anonymously. No one has asked for anything. We didn't have any money when we came; in fact we had large debts, and people here and elsewhere, who made their money by working very hard, some of them for their whole lives, gave us what they could, each person, small or large. No one is going to be thanked in a big way. There's no building here to put a plaque with their name. There are no banquets. They knew that they were giving without any need for anyone knowing.

And the people who brought us here, those of you who were there, does it strike you how they just appeared and disappeared quietly, with nothing? They didn't ask for anything. The owners of this property proposed the idea that we could stay here freely. They have tied up large amounts of their money and land for years, and no one ever asked for anything. They just anonymously went home. The people who planned all the things here came from around the world at their own expense, and they continue to come. Nobody knows they're here or that they're coming. They're not going to get any recognition. And they're spending all their own time and money.

Many people send us things. We have a rule that we're not allowed to know who sent them. We received, for example, so many piles of warm clothing that finally we had to ask, "Please don't send any more. There's no place to put it." Sometimes we see the tags, and they come from many countries: some from Ireland, the Holy Isle, and some from the Far East, some from New York, some from California.

There's a little project to bake things and send them here for our altars. We have great fun trying to guess who baked this one. Some cookies I've seen since I was very young, so I know [laughs]. There are also not many people who make Tibetan doughnuts like someone *does. Many people who are sitting around you, or who are not here, send them anonymously. It's like an epidemic of anonymous goodness. And because one person doesn't need to get famous, the next person says,*

"That's a good thing." And so it has spread, and so is the goodness of so many people working. We don't even know who's taking care of us. We knew a year ago. People come and fix things. We leave for the day. We walk away, and we're not even sure who did it. They know that, and still they want to help.

So I'm very proud to be near so many people like that. The people in retreat here are doing it for the right reasons. Nobody much knows they're here, and the few people who know think they're odd. [Laughs]. They have many lonely nights. The hardest part of the loneliness, I think, must be that no one knows you're sick today. No one knows you cried for a few hours because you were lonely. And no one perhaps will ever know that you spent a whole week fighting a doubt, or some kind of emotion, and couldn't sleep. And they are doing everything completely anonymously. This is the right way.

We spoke the first day about how important it is to find a great teacher. When you are near a living human being who is good at what you hope to learn, there are silent transmissions of knowledge and goodness that occur that can't be duplicated by books or computers or videos or tape recordings. And then we said that each person should have the courage to find the best teacher there is, and should be brave enough to pester them and learn from them.

After that we talked about emptiness, which in this case means that if you are trying to learn anything like dance or music or scripture, as you look down at that book or that piano or your feet, everything you see is not what you thought it was. It's not your feet down there. It's not a piano out there. It's not a book whose edge you feel in your hands. These are images created by your mind.

Where do these images come from? When you feel a book in your hands, it's really just a bunch of random atoms or pieces of matter, and then your brain organizes them, and you think you feel a book. Your brain is forced to do so by seeds in your mind—we'll call them "imprints" today, or "seeds." They were planted there in the past by your mind, which is beginningless and carries seeds from year to year. They were planted there when you were good or when you were not good to someone else.

This is precisely why every great religion urges us to be good. When you are good, you plant a seed in your mind, and later your mind thinks it sees the edge of a good book. This is reality. These images are not just little random pictures. All together, they are your world and your body and your mind. This is where everything really comes from.

And so we said that if that's true, then every time you get good at something that you're trying to learn, it has nothing to do with that thing. Why do you think some people take piano lessons and can play well? Why do you think other people fail? Why do you think some people try yoga or some exercise and become healthy and strong, and others try and break their legs and give up? Why do you think so many people try to read the great books and only a few understand?

It indicates that the knowledge is not in the book. It indicates that yoga or some other exercise is not really what made you healthy. It indicates that it wasn't really your teacher who made you a great piano player. These are all images coming from your own mind because of good things you did to someone in the past.

So if you were my age and it was time to learn something new, it would seem that learning how to be good to others, learning how to serve others, would be the most intelligent thing to learn. Then anything you hoped to learn, you could learn quickly. You could master anything. First master serving others, then all things come automatically.

So we have to find a teacher who can teach us the key to and the source of all happiness, of all learning, of all success, be it business or health. That's a teacher who can show us how to serve others. So I urge you when you try to find a teacher, don't think, "I want to find a meditation teacher," or "I want to find a Buddhism teacher," or "I want to find a scripture teacher." I think you should try to find the teacher who is very good at serving others and who understands that all things come from that, because all things come from your mind.

Emptiness means things are not what you thought they were. Yoga or other exercise is empty of functioning to make you healthy. It doesn't. Gasoline is empty of having any power to move a car. Food is empty of any power to make you strong. All things come from how you treated others in the past.

"Prove it."

Many people choke on food and die. I saw one. It means that food doesn't necessarily make you healthy. It is like a blank screen, and you see in the food what your past actions force you to see.

Then we spoke about some qualities of a good teacher. It was ninety-something. Everyone froze to death and hopefully, as you sniffled this morning, you made a list. I hope you have it in your hand. We were supposed to write down five good qualities we see in a person who is teaching us anything, and five qualities which they don't seem very strong in and we wish they were better. It's very important today, because we're going to talk about how you can find a perfect teacher. How can you find one who has only the good qualities and not the bad qualities on your list?

First or all, you must understand that if you see a good quality in a person, in a teacher or anyone else, it's a reflection of your own mind. You have had that quality, and it planted a seed in you, and so you see it now in someone else. If you see a single praiseworthy quality in another person, you should pat yourself on the back. Equally so, if you see any negative quality in another person, it's only because you have a seed to see that in your own mind, which was planted when you had that negative quality. And it's never been any other way. On one hand, it's very gladdening to know that all the goodness you see is a reflection of what you have been. And it's very saddening to know that all the bad things you ever see in others are a reflection of what you have been.

I say "have been" because you can change it. So today I think it's important to talk about how do you keep the good qualities that you see rolling and how can we stop the bad things we see?

I'd like to talk about the good things first. In case I die halfway through we've said the good things first. People ask me, "Can you see your future lives? [Crying.] Can you see your past lives?" And people say, "Can you see my past life?"

I have the honor to know a holy person named Salim. Once we were driving in a car. I was wondering out loud, I think, why he had such great faith. And he said, "It can't be me, Geshe-la. I think it was Joe" [laughs]. He kept talking about "Joe."

Finally I was ashamed to admit, "I don't know; who's Joe?"

"Oh, Geshe-hla, Joe was my past life. I don't know exactly but he must have been a great guy."

I can't see your past lives directly. But I can say with absolute certainty that there was a holy being, a great saint, who spent their whole life, day and night, doing good for others. And on her deathbed, she made a solemn prayer to be born to serve others in a good place with good teachers.

And that was you, because you wouldn't be here otherwise. You are one in a million. I swear that's true. In their dying breath, they pushed their mind into this world, and you grew up a special person. In your school you were different. In your family you were different. You had instincts about things that were special. As you grew up, you were asking questions; you were wondering about special things. And then somehow you found, not just this tradition, but I think each person here found special truth in different traditions: many books, churches, temples, and synagogues. You found special books. You had unusual friends. You had special teachers come to you up to now. And all this time you were sort of proud, thinking, "I'm special. I'm so lucky to have these special people around me. I'm so lucky to have found the books I've found, parents and friends who were different."

But now you have to wake up. That was Joe's work. You have to realize that you and I haven't done anything so special that we could create the image of a Dalai Lama on our planet. We haven't done anything so special that we could walk into a bookstore at will and pick up fifty books on Jesus or Lord Buddha. That was Joe. You and I have eaten and slept and been jealous and angry at other people and judged them our whole lives. What have we done to create holy lamas like Khen Rinpoche or Zopa Rinpoche? Be honest; we haven't done that many good things. That was Joe. We are living off somebody else's credit card. It has a spending limit. Those imprints which you received on his or her dying breath are wearing out.

Do you know who Ling Rinpoche was, teacher of the Dalai Lama? Do you know Geshe Losang Ludrung, abbot of Sera Mey? Did you know Geshe Ngawang Dhargye, holy lama? Did you meet Geshe Rabten, who brought Buddhism to the west? Did you meet Lama Yeshe, holy being? And there were dozens of others. No. Why? They are passed from this world. *[Cries.]* Why? Because our imprints wore out.

These beings don't die, and you won't die. People don't die. Animals don't die. It's that the seeds in their minds to see themselves wear out. The seeds you have in your mind to see the few great masters left are wearing out. His Holiness is getting old.

So when you look down at your list and you see five good qualities, you can thank Joe. And you can be afraid you will lose these five. They don't last forever. They are imprints. Every minute the Dalai Lama lives, you have lost countless days of work by Joe, and Joe's Joe, and Joe's Joe's Joe. You have to realize you are living off credit that someone else worked for.

You were born on an escalator, and it's moving down fast. You don't even know. Every breath you take is hundreds of good deeds done by Joe. It's hard to believe. Just to stay even, you'd have to turn around and run up the escalator at the speed of a Lama Zopa, and we are nothing like that. He works day and night to help others. He doesn't sleep.

"Oh, he takes a special pill."

I tried to get one. Khen Rinpoche said they don't exist.

The reason Lama Zopa doesn't sleep is that he can't bear to waste another hour of helping others. These people are maybe running up the escalator fast enough to stay even with what Joe was. We are standing there like fools, and we are about to hit the bottom.

The saddest thing is we don't even realize it. Those of you who are under thirty or thirty-five, be honest. Have you really done anything so great that you could suddenly bump into holy Lama Khen Rinpoche, or the great holy books you have read? Were you so different from the other kids at school? Did you help thousands of people? That was all done by another person. You'll lose it.

The sad thing is you won't even know or care. Because the imprint to care is wearing out also. You'll come out of your retreat, and the mom or dad in five years will say, "She or he finally woke up. They are working and they're going to buy a house and they stopped all that foolishness."

And the sad thing is, it will be true. You will be standing facing a bookshelf: "What were these books for? I don't remember. It used to be important. But I need place to put the new washer-drier. I won't throw them out, because I remember there was something important. I'll keep them in a box in the basement. That was when I was young. I was so idealistic. I thought I could save the world." The imprints to care wore out.

I studied with a rabbi; I never told you that, in Brooklyn. He was almost ninety, and his name was (Addisan). He said one day, "I think the president of the United States should always be someone under thirty. I don't know why, but only people under thirty really want to save the world."

The reason is Joe's hard work wears off. So when you look at the good qualities, you have to try to keep them. You are creating any good thing you see in your teacher. You have to try to keep working, or those qualities will disappear. "I studied with him for a few years and slowly I began to see flaws."

There was a student of Lord Buddha named Lekhar. He stayed with Lord Buddha, a perfect being, for twelve years. Finally he quit, because his imprints wore off. People would ask him, "Is He enlightened?" He'd say, "I don't see a single good quality in this person. Except one. He has this funny light shining around his head."

Jesus was sitting having dinner. I think it was with a publican. A publican was a traitor of the Jewish people who agreed to collect taxes for the Roman conquering army. And he used to hang out with whores and publicans and other evil people. People couldn't believe it.

They were having dinner. A woman came in and fell at her feet before Jesus. Then she opened up a precious box of white marble, I think, and massaged precious, priceless oil into his hair. The disciples were shocked. "How can you let this woman do this? This money could have saved the lives of many poor people."

He said, "You don't understand what's happening here. This woman's name will be spoken of thousands of years from now. She will go down in history. She is putting ointment on the body of a man soon to die. This is my death ointment. You don't understand."

At that moment, one of the disciples made up his mind to be sure that this man was captured and killed. He couldn't believe the corruption he saw, because his imprints had worn out.

So what to do if you see something wrong in a teacher? Some people say, "Just look the other way." But if you're the kind of person who has come to a teacher to learn holy things, you're not the type to look away. Sooner or later, you can't look away.

Some people say, "The guru is perfect. You're a bad person. Just stop seeing what you see."

"How can I stop seeing what I see? I see something wrong. And I know I'm a bad person, and that's why I came to this teacher. And if the teacher's a bad person, how am I going to become a good person?" It doesn't work to tell people good disciples don't see bad things in their gurus.

Some people say, "Confront them."

"You gave a stirring talk six months ago about not abusing our bodies by eating badly, and I remember you used to eat three bowls of ice cream in one sitting." And more serious confrontations.

But it's my experience that things don't change. They will eat their ice cream in private next time.

Some people say, "Just move on. Find a better teacher."

It's a little bit like divorcing wife number one and finding number two. It's a little like quitting your job because you don't like someone there. It's a little bit like moving to a better city. It never ends, and you know it. There are very few people with two wives, because they're already used to moving on. The problem with moving on is that you carry the cause for what you saw in the first wife in your mind. Whatever you didn't like in the first wife or first husband will appear in the second one shortly. Whatever you didn't like about your old job will resurface at the new job. Whatever problem you had with your old neighborhood will appear in your new one, because they're coming from your own mind. It doesn't work to move on.

Some people say, "Compromise. Make the best of it. He or she is a pretty good teacher."

I don't think a person with Joe's seeds in their mind is going to be satisfied with a compromise for very long. I don't think you should compromise. I don't think you should make the best of something bad with a teacher. Your life is at stake.

The happiness of many people is at stake.

Some people say, "Take the flaw you see and turn it into an opportunity. Find a silver lining in the clouds."

I think it's wise advice, but it doesn't fix anything. It's like saying, "You're blind. Try to make the best of it. You can become a great musician." That's true. But I'd rather have eyes.

Finally, some people say, "It's a test. The guru is testing you. The guru is angry today and hitting you to see if you can master the art of patience."

This only works for a certain while. "I've been tested now for thirty years by your anger. I'm tired of testing. Either I've failed already or it's not going to work. Can you just appear as a perfect being?"

I, at some level, say no to all of those options. If things are empty of any quality of their own, if everything I see in another person is a reflection of seeds in my mind, then, god damn it, I will change the seeds. And I can see something perfect.

Don't mind the rain. I was in Thailand. I went to meditate in an open square with about a hundred lay people. It poured, and no one moved an inch. I was embarrassed and my suit was soaked. Finally I left. I missed whatever they said.

So how can I change the things I see? If you see a teacher who is, for example, obsessed with money, it is because in the past you yourself were obsessed with money, and you put a seed in your mind to be obsessed with money. It's always something similar.

If you want to identify the seed in your mind that makes you see something bad in another person—I'm talking about teachers, but it applies to your wife or husband or children or your dog—then you have to think, "I'm seeing a teacher who is obsessed with money. It comes from being obsessed with money in the past.

"But I've never been obsessed with money."

These seeds can be very old. You have to understand that these seeds could come from Joe's time. You had the seed.

67

This explains why good people suffer. They have a seed; they weren't always good. You have to remove that seed. How? If your teacher is obsessed with money, then you must take special care to be generous. And it must always be for others. Because it's by doing things to others, good or bad, that these seeds are planted.

So look down the list at the five things you don't like about a teacher, the five things they lack, and fix them. The process is unilateral. You don't have to say a thing to the teacher. Quietly, purposefully, with great knowledge of the key to all things, be generous.

I want to try to impress on you that this really works. If you had a teacher who seemed to be obsessed with money, and if you truly with a good heart try to be generous to others to remove that seed, you will see a transformation. Perhaps the teacher will call you in one day and say, "You know, I've decided. I used to charge a lot of money for classes. I've changed my ways. I was greedy. Now I'm never going to do that again." Your seed to see them as being obsessed with money wore out, and you wore it out. This is true dharma practice. You don't have to put up with all those other compromises. You can change reality itself.

The exciting thing is that you can even change what happened in the past. For example, if the teacher seemed to be a cheapskate, always chintzing on food, always grubbing to save a dime or nickel at the store in the past for years, then they might call you up into their room one day and say, "Maybe you noticed I've been grubby for the last five years, trying to save a nickel or dime. Maybe you thought I was being cheap. Well, I've collected sixty thousand dollars, and today I want you to write out a bank transfer to India. We are going to make a fund to feed all the poor monks."

It's interesting and exciting to know that event didn't happen until you were generous. And then, because you were generous, you killed the seed in your mind to see your teacher as being greedy, and an actual event, which already took place, transformed before your eyes. It's wonderful. You can control your destiny. You can make anything happen. Finally.

Sometimes the result of wiping out the imprint will appear in another person. If you have teacher who's not very knowledgeable but who's very kind, and if you try to wipe out the imprint to have a teacher who's not very knowledgeable, then either the first teacher will suddenly reveal their knowledge, or another teacher will appear in your life to complement the kindness of the first teacher. So the first teacher has become two beings. Are they the same person? I think it's good to think that way. Either way, you now have a teacher who has knowledge.

How do you get a teacher like that? How do you wipe out a seed in your mind to have a teacher who's not very knowledgeable? You must preserve knowledge for others. It has been one of the greatest frustrations of my life in the last ten years to teach day after day and to see the most talented people in front of me feeding off of Joe, and not making a very great effort to preserve, or to learn and master what I was teaching. A few did, and they worked very hard. One of the people on the staff here recently finished, I think, a six-hundred-page manuscript of every single word of a very holy teaching that happened. And another person finished two huge beautiful manuscripts of teachings we received from a great lama in India.

But these are not typical. You will lose the seeds you have in your mind to meet a knowledgeable teacher, because you're making no special effort to make sure that others have this knowledge. Joe did, which is why you have the fortune to be exposed to great holy knowledge, but you're doing nothing to keep that imprint alive. It will die. You will lose that teacher. Not because they left or died, or because you left, but because the imprint wore out. The imprint to have a knowledgeable teacher takes decades of hard work.

"Are you saying that if I were to change my ways and make very great efforts to help other people learn holy knowledge, then suddenly new teachers would pop up in my life?"

Exactly!

"But the old Tibetan masters are gone."

Don't be naïve. These beings don't have to look like Tibetans. They don't have to look like a monk or nun. They don't have to look like a lama. If you were seriously working for others in the early part of your life, trying to share holy knowledge, trying to preserve holy knowledge, then in the latter part of your life they could appear as anyone.

"Are you saying such a person might be surrounded by holy teachers who appeared like just young Americans?"

Exactly.

"You're saying they could teach that person the path to holy enlightenment?"

Exactly.

"But they look like normal American young people."

To whom?

"To me."

You don't have imprints; you didn't work that hard. And you will lose what you have. You have to do these things for others. Save knowledge. Preserve it. Make sure it's ready to hand on to others. Dedicate it with an act of truth.

"What's an act of truth?"

"I dedicate the work I put in on this manuscript of a holy teaching to always meeting holy teachers in the future, because I understand this is only a seed in my mind, and I pray—I dedicate—this good deed to seeing holy teachers in the future. Because I understand they're empty. I will only see what my seeds force me to see."

This is extremely powerful. There's a big difference between preserving some kind of holy knowledge for others because you like to, and preserving holy knowledge for others with the knowledge that everything is blank and you will only see what you see because of the seeds you put in your mind. To plant the seeds purposely is the holiest act a person can do. Joe knew how to do it. You forgot. Joe forgot to plant a seed for remembering. I'm not kidding. It's typical. Or Joe would be somewhere else now.

This is very, very powerful. The simple knowledge that you can destroy a negative quality you see in your teacher by destroying any small tendency you have towards that quality, and the decision to try, can destroy the imprint immediately in some cases. We can call those "soft imprints." You don't even have to carry out your plan. The decision to try (is enough).

"I have a teacher who's very jealous."

Then you stop being jealous.

"I believe you. I'm not so jealous, but what little jealousy I have, I will stop it, I'll try to catch myself, and I will dedicate it to wipe out that seed in my mind. Are you telling me that suddenly that teacher would change?"

Yes. And if the imprint in your mind is soft, it will change just by deciding to try to stop your own jealousy.

But I warn you equally, to be honest, that there are hard imprints, concrete imprints, iron imprints. They take weeks or months or sometimes years of your life. Joe was a very jealous holy man, and unfortunately he planted many seeds to see jealousy in my mind. And I have to carry on Joe's good work. You might have to work for years on a hard imprint, by fighting your own small jealousies. But it works. I think I can say honestly that if you understand this method, which is called *paramita*, the six perfections—it's what makes them perfections—and if you really understand it, then your reality will change radically in a few months. But if it takes longer, if I may point out, we don't have a choice. Are you going to live the rest of your life compromising? Do you want to live around jealous people the rest of your life, and die and see more later? Do you want to live around teachers and wives and brothers and friends who have flaws forever? Do you want forever to be a person who has these flaws? We don't have a choice. If the imprints are soft or hard, we have to clean them from our own minds.

Please enjoy some refreshments, and we'll start, and it won't be very long after.

I was a little hesitant to teach you this special method of creating your perfect teacher, for obvious reasons. People might ask you, "What did Geshe Michael talk about in Arizona?" And not remembering very well, you'd say, "He said any guru who has a big flaw, it's my fault." No, you must try to remember. I'm talking about an extremely radical alteration of your reality, done consciously and purposely—cold logic. You change them, because what they are is a result of an imprint in your own mind.

"If I have a teacher who's a cheapskate, and if I am generous and I, as you said, I must do it for others and I must consciously dedicate it to seeing that teacher change, will the teacher realize they've changed?"

No. It's very important. It's subtle, but you must know it to do this practice successfully. Small acts of generosity are enough, if you dedicate them with an act of truth. "If it's true that I gave up half of my doughnut to this other guy who I didn't even like, then may my teacher's cheapness go away." It's enough; it works.

Is the teacher aware of this process? You have to understand, no. What they see from their side we don't know. Maybe they were trying to help us, but I'm not even suggesting that you try to believe that. It doesn't really matter. Until the day we can read their minds, we'll never know, and it doesn't matter.

"Are you saying that just an ordinary young American person can walk up to you, if you've spent your life trying to preserve the dharma, and every sentence they say shoves you into enlightenment, and they don't even realize it?"

Exactly. This is emptiness. If you're a great person, if your mind is holy enough, you'll get it.

"Then aren't you just fooling yourself? They don't even know they're doing it?"

No, *you're* fooling yourself.

"Which is real, the person who doesn't know they're shoving you into enlightenment or you seeing them shoving you into enlightenment? Which is right? What are they really?"

Oh, you don't understand emptiness. They aren't really either one. There's no base condition; there's no standard reality; there's no starting point. There's only what they see and you see.

"Are you suggesting we just believe everyone is a holy teacher?"

No. If you have planted the seeds in your mind, you will believe, because they will be. And if you haven't planted the seed in your mind by helping others, serving others, you'll never see it no matter how many times I tell you this person is an angel.

I want to be very clear that I'm not making excuses for corrupt teachers. Jesus said, "They have their reward." What did he mean? Corrupt teachers want to take advantage of their students. They are hoping to get famous or rich. So maybe they have some pleasure from a student, or they get some money, or they get famous for a short time, and then they experience all the suffering of pleasure, and money, and fame. It's suffering because it's meaningless. Their reward is what they hoped for, and it's hell. I don't mean they go to some fiery place, which they do. I mean the result that they hoped for, some brief pleasure, is itself a kind of suffering, and that becomes apparent. How much can you eat in one life? How much money can you spend? How many pairs of shoes can you buy before you figure it out?

Think carefully of all the bad qualities you see on the right side of your sheet. If they have come from my own mind, if I remove them by avoiding even the slightest tendency towards cheapness or other qualities myself, what will happen eventually? If you take the worst five and clean them, and then you take the second worst five and clean them, eventually you'll have a perfect teacher; and guess what? You'll be perfect.

So the magic of empty teachers is that in the exercise of creating your perfect match made in heaven, that you become perfect. The teaching is finished before you start. The whole process of seeking your perfect lama has made you perfect. You slide into tantric paradise automatically. It's magic; it's holy. That's why it's the first step of all great scriptures.

Now you know how to do it right. You're not supposed to be an unthinking slave of the guru. You're not supposed to pretend you don't see flaws where they are glaring to anyone. You have to come and use the guru and their flaws to make yourself perfect.

Go home tonight and take your sheet. This is your homework. There's a column by each good quality and bad quality that says "T.D.F.O.," what to do for others. What to do for others?

"To be honest, I don't see that my teacher treats his students equally." That one is on the right side, and not on the left side. "I don't see that he treats all his students equally like a lawn of grass would treat all feet equally."

Then you write in, according to your own logic what you have to do to rip out that seed from your mind. It will somehow involve treating other people equally. It took perhaps thousands of years to plant the seeds in your mind to see a person not treat others equally. Luckily it doesn't take thousands of years to remove the seed. Just in your own small way from day to day when you have a chance to treat others equally, do so, and dedicate it purposely, consciously. Sit down and say, "I dedicate this tiny act of equality to see that bad quality leave my teacher." And it will. Keep the list with you and work on those five bad qualities.

On the good side, if you have a teacher who is knowledgeable, then write, "To do for others is to learn well what my teacher says." Record it in your notebooks well. Write it down, for the sake of your own students. Don't say, "I'm not interested in that subject," or, "I heard that before."

I had the great fortune to see His Holiness speak in New York. I looked around, and some people were making a few notes. There was a man on the stage in the row of monks making furious notes. It was Lama Zopa Rinpoche. He doesn't need to take notes, but he's afraid to forget some precious gem he has received. And therefore he is fortunate enough even now to have wonderful teachers. So on the good side put something for yourself to do so you don't lose Joe's hard work.

Then on both sides, there should be something written to do for others and dedicate to find a perfect teacher.

Okay. That's homework. Don't forget.

Fourth Day:

Sunday, March 11, 2001

Why is the Teacher perfect?

IV.

Vajradhara, Keeper of the Diamond,
Has come again."
But how can we be sure?
See and feel the stone.

There is space
And it is place
They live and die without it.

There is wind
And it is motion
They live and die without it.

There is water
And it is moisture
They live and die without it.

There is fire
And it is warmth

They live and die without it.

There is earth
And it stands up
They live and die without it.

Twilight worlds
Beneath a rose petal
On the open sea
In the dark of night

On the petal one diamond
So none less is sent;
No boy for the job,
No fool for a Dalai Lama.

He comes for the final step
And She is Vajradhara
For You are the coming Buddha,
You are the coming Buddha.

We'll do a very brief meditation.

Okay, we'll start. There's a good Irishman walking around handing out stones. Please close your eyes and take one. At the end if there's extra, please take them if you like for friends. They're from inside the "tsam," or the retreat boundary. We'll need the stones later for the teaching.

I was hoping to clarify some things before we start. We talked about how much a person should meditate, and I wanted to repeat it to make sure it's clear. If you are a working person with an outside job, and I know because I did it for almost twenty years, you have maybe about two free hours a day that you could either meditate or study the holy books, or help the Dharma projects with administrative work. And I'd like to make it very, very clear that whatever time you have available each day, half should go to meditation, not less than that. And I'm speaking about each day, so you can't collect up missed meditation periods and do them on Sunday.

You will sense your other good work slipping, and you'll be afraid that maybe when Geshe Michael gets out of retreat, he'll be upset that these things didn't get done. Don't think like that. Let them slide a little bit, and if you see each other missing meditation periods, you can quote me, and force them to sit down. Someone has to do it for me.

Then if you are working, say as a caretaker here, and spending maybe eight hours or something working, or if you are a full time worker in Dharma work, then I think the ratio should be two to one. If you spend six hours working on driving around and shopping, or cooking, then I think at least two, and better three, hours meditating, practicing. It means the retreatants may have to have canned soup more often, and that's fine.

Please, I think I speak for all of us, we don't want you to hurt your meditation and your samadhi. You can't help anyone if you do some kind of Dharma work, or even study, and your mind is not calm and collected and peaceful. If you find that you feel stressed or overwhelmed by the demands of some kind of Dharma job or study, then you should reduce the job and the study. The state of your mind comes first.

I hope that each person can get a copy of the tape recording of the sixth class of the sixth course of this school, which is about the direct perception of emptiness in the Diamond Cutter Sutra. There are several tapes around. The first one, in the basement of Hells Kitchen with the dogs barking, is good. The next couple are good: Massachusetts, when Kieran came to us, and also Australia is good. Vajrapani is very good. Bodhgaya is great.

Then in your free time—I think it would be fun on Sunday mornings—if you can just turn it on, even while you are eating breakfast. Listen once.

Another thing I wanted to suggest was it's much easier to do your practices regularly if you have someone like a practice partner to do them with. Especially if your lama has said you must do this practice five or six days a week. If it's something new, it would be helpful to find another person who is interested in the same practices, and you can support each other.

Try to find a person who is disciplined. Try to find a person who is on your level or higher, and then you will support each other. It's very important. For those of you who are married, this is very good. You can catch each other. When one person is lazy, the other should say, "We're going to do it anyway." If one person wants to eat a big breakfast before meditation and the other should say, "No, let's eat afterwards."

Oftentimes here, it clouds over. Well, not often, just when you come. But there's this sTrange phenomenon here. When it's mealtime, we hear the truck or car start up to bring us our meals, and the saliva starts to come out. There's a special connection between the door of that vehicle and thunderstorms. As soon as the door slams when they get here, the heaviest rain starts to fall on them. And we wince when we hear the door and imagine them. And then we hear footsteps coming up to the food box, which is outside the fence.

We never see them. We are keeping a good retreat, and we don't see other people. Maybe once in awhile a dentist or some very fine traditional exercise teachers of ancient customs come. But we haven't seen the main kind people who take care of us since we started, and we don't speak or communicate otherwise. You can imagine that we have a very subtle sign language developing, and just looking in each other's faces we know what's going on. But the silence has been very good. I don't include laughing; you know that.

Then you hear them tromping up. They sound tired, from the sound of their feet, and you have a tremendous urge to drop what you are doing. We do only three things: we meditate and we memorize the nutrition facts on cans and jars, because we have nothing else to read. Or we might be humming a TV theme show song. I don't know why they flood into your mind.

But you get this urge to run out and open the door of the fence and give them a big hug for all the hard work. So we all thought you could help us. There are those three holy ladies; I bet they're in front somewhere. And during the break or after class, you should give them a big hug, and it's from us, OK?

I'm not kidding—lots of hugs. You can squish them. And there's this quiet Canadian guy and another quiet Irish guy who are always coming with a hammer, climbing up on the top of the yurts, risking life and limb to keep us warm or cool. I think they need a hug too. And I don't know whose helping them, because we haven't seen anyone, but they need hugs too. And that's in the break or afterwards.

*And while you're at it, there's a director, and he's nervous. He's got a lot of respon-
sibility. Now he has to keep samadhi too. He needs a hug from you. And while
he's flying around the world saving people, his wife as usual is stuck with the two
children and all the work, and she and the kids need a bigger hug.*

*So now you have, I think nine or ten hugs you should give. While you're at it, if
you ever meet the kind owners of this land, I think you should give them and their
family a big hug. While you're at it, if you meet the people who first brought us
here, they need hugs too.*

*There are these beautiful cows. At first we were annoyed—they interrupted the
meditation, "MOOOO!" Now we love them; it's like comic relief. When you are
having a bad thought you hear, "Mmmrrrrrr." When you are doing well you hear,
"MORE! MORE!" They're sort of shy—you could just wave to them.*

*And the birds and the other creatures. We have many creatures who come now
to be with us. Happily, they don't seem afraid anymore. All kinds, like moles
and beautiful kangaroo rats. There's a beautiful red flicker, a woodpecker, who
actually sleeps at night in one of the alcoves of the yurt. And if you think about it
when you're eating your refreshments, then throw a little bit on the ground around.
They'll get it. I believe there are spirits and protectors among them.*

*While you're at it, if you meet one of the kind sponsors....There's this beautiful,
powerful woman from Tucson; there's a shy man from Santa Cruz. There's an
equally shy man, an ex-rugby player, I think, from the northeast. There's an ex-
football player from New York. There's a lady who wants to become a nun, from
New York. There are many people from Singapore and Australia. If you happen to
see one of them in the break or after class or three months from now, then please
give them a big hug from us.*

*If you run into the people who built our places, or the people who continue to send
us wonderful things, like things for our altars—incense, candles, cookies—then
give them a big hug. I think any moms in the audience should get a big hug too.
You have to be our representatives. And any children, no matter how precocious.*

If you meet the crafters of the great sword here or in Ireland someday, you should

79

give them a big hug. If you meet the man who foolishly agreed to take over all the classes and administration in New York, who has found out what a headache it is, who's lost all his income to that cause, there and in Connecticut, you should give him a big hug. He needs it now.

And there's a guy like him took over the computer project to save the holy books in this world, and he's probably pretty stressed now too, and he needs a big hug.

And the guy who didn't know a word of Tibetan and agreed to do all the creation of tools for that, he's probably wondering what the heck to do. He needs a hug.

The bolshoi ruski chelovyek doktor....If you see a big Russian doctor guy, give him a hug. If you see the lady doctor from Santa Cruz who also treats us, later, give her a hug too. She should have two hugs from each. And all the Western monks and nuns, who are so brave to try to keep vows in this country, they should get proper, respectful hugs.

Every six months we get a couple of weeks to goof off—this is a monastery custom. We read cheap novels and listen to rock and roll. There are a couple of people who send us our contrabands, and they should get hugs too. And if you meet one of our holy Lamas, you should make three hug-like prostrations. Or if you meet anyone who is helping to take care of them. Or the people who put out nice books of teachings, here or elsewhere, and send them to us.

So, I'm not kidding, I'm serious. Please do it during the break, or after the class. If someone is not here, and there are many people who are helping who I didn't mention, you should give them a big hug from us. Don't forget. I think all the retreatants should get a hug, but maybe later—or they can give each other hugs.

We spoke about what a huge difference it is between trying to learn something on your own and really becoming a master in the hands of a great master. And then we spoke about how you shouldn't be afraid to look for this master, and approach them, and find a way to be at their side. Then we spoke about emptiness. It means that, in actuality, everything you see around you is an image organized by your own mind. There are really only colors, random colors, around you. The ground itself is really only random sensations that you have. And your own mind organizes them into objects.

Your mind is forced to organize them into objects by mental seeds that were planted earlier by you when you did something kind or something unkind to others. Your entire reality, from earth to sky, and all the people you've ever met, are images formed by your mind.

Does that mean they're not real? No, it explains why they're real, and it opens the greatest opportunity of all time. If you know about these things, you can shape your own future. From pancakes to paradise, you can consciously make it happen. But as you may have noticed, it all hinges on how you treat others.

So we said that no matter what you hope to learn, whether it's music, building, painting, dancing, or being a doctor, if you succeed, this is only an image in your mind that came from being kind to others in that way. If you succeed in business, if you reap large profits, if your company grows into something huge, it is only because you have been generous to others in the past.

And so we said it made a lot of sense to try to find a teacher who could teach you the best ways to be kind to others. You should seek a master of serving others. It's hard, and there are countless levels of serving others. If you reach the highest levels, everything else that you ever hope to learn or succeed at will come effortlessly.

Then we had a long freezing class about the qualities of a master—how to recognize a master, what to look for, and what to strive for. Then we had a hard class, because it was hailing, about the magic of empty teachers. Teachers are like everything else, they have been created. They are images in your mind that come from seeds you planted before. And I tried to stress that you can manipulate those seeds; you can remove bad ones by being good to others in the same way. For example, if your teacher seems more interested in money than teaching, you can remove that perception by being generous to others yourself.

This is a very unusual, novel way to think. It almost seems impossible. I propose unabashedly that it is the only way to think. If you see it, if you try it—if all things come from whether you were kind or unkind to others in the past—give it a try; see if it works.

I'll say something very radical; you remember. Gasoline doesn't make cars go, your behavior to others in the past does. If you have not been generous to travelers in the past, it doesn't matter if you have gasoline in the car, something will break.

The gasoline by itself does not have the power to move the car. What's moving the car is your behavior in the past to others.

Get used to it. Try to imagine what this means. Things are images. They are only coming from your past love or dislike of others. This is why every great spiritual teacher in history, from Moses on, has begged people to be good to each other. It's the only way to make things work, because all things come from that.

I propose, and try to remember, that no object in this world affects another object. Matches don't create fire. Food doesn't make you go. The very motion of the sun and stars is something you are creating from your past actions towards others. And therefore, anything can happen.

The last quality we listed for a great teacher was a perfect match made in heaven. You should try to find the perfect teacher, the perfect match for you. What is the action that we can take if we don't have a perfect match? How can we make a seed in our minds to see and meet the perfect one for us? I'd like to talk about that today.

All the Buddhist holy books say the same thing. There are two kinds of books, the open books which anyone is allowed to read, and the secret books. And they all say the same thing. Your teacher is Vajradhara. They say your teacher is Vajradhara. Vajradhara has come again into the world for you.

"Who's Vajradhara?"

As I describe Vajradhara, you can think of Jesus or Moses; it doesn't matter. Try to grasp the main idea in whichever way is good for you. The holy books of Tibet, I would say a hundred thousand of them, they all say, "Your teacher is Jesus come again into the world to help you, alone. Your teacher is Moses come once more to help you."

"Who's Vajradhara?"

Lord Buddha, who's only one of the great expressions of holiness that have come to this world, gave three great groups of teachings. Those of you who are familiar with the three turnings of the wheel, I'm not speaking about that. Lord Buddha appeared in three radically different forms in this world.

First he came in the form of a monk, a simple hermit monk. He gave his first teachings in this form. He said, "All things are suffering, there's a way out, here's how." And he taught twelve links, the causes and effects that chain us to this suffering. In the form of a monk, he said everyone should try to become a monk and move into a cell in a monastery or under a tree. Everyone should stay quietly by themselves and try to meditate, and over the course of millions of years you may become enlightened.

Then later, Lord Buddha changed his form entirely. He appeared as what we call a bodhisattva monk and taught what we call the perfections, how to serve others. "Don't stay under your tree all day. Do your practice, meditate, and then get up and serve others."

A monk living by *vinaya* as it was taught in the first form, for example, is not even allowed to pray or meditate together with people who are not full monks. In his second form, Lord Buddha said, "Now I want you to go to the cities to find people and help them on the path. They don't have to be monks, and you should pray with them." And he said, "This path is faster, and this path helps more people."

The first path is a foundation for the second. We don't reject the first path, but the second is an evolution of the first path. Naturally some people on the first path who were still babies thought the second path was a little weird. But eventually all people come up to the second path.

Then Lord Buddha appeared in his third form. This is the form in which he actually lives in his own paradise. He had long beautiful black hair. He wore the silken clothing of the angels. He had jewels on him. He showed his true form to a few people, and he said, "There's a better way. There's a faster way. I am showing you what I look like in my own home. I want you to learn how to be like that. In one lifetime, in this life, before you get old or die, you can move into a paradise. And from that headquarters, you can serve the living creatures on countless planets."

This form is Vajradhara. "Vajra" means "diamond." "Dhara" means "the one who holds the Diamond." In Tibetan, it's Dorje Chang. And so the Buddha taught special secret teachings for many years, and still we have almost fifteen hundred teachings from ancient India on these secret ways, by Lord Buddha and those whom he taught as Vajradhara.

"What was Vajradhara's main teaching?" You should know that.

I used to sit with the holiest Lama Khen *[crying]* Rinpoche in his room. He kept a television there, I think to make me feel comfortable. He especially likes the Winter Olympics, and especially the ice-skaters. And I don't know if you know, they have a custom when they compete. First they do very boring exercises, like circles, that they never show on TV. Then later they get to do their special figure skating to music. They combine great skill with beauty, and Rinpoche was overwhelmed with the beauty. And then there's a custom that if you win the gold medal, then you get to come out for an encore.

If you win the medal, you get to come out and do a performance to a song that you really like, not a classical song. And I think we enjoyed that the most, because they're not nervous. They're not trying to beat anyone, and they are totally relaxed. They've already won the medal and they are skating for the sake of skating. They are dancing for the sake of dance. They are showing beauty for the sake of beauty. No pressure.

And so try to imagine one of those anonymous hard-working master coaches behind the little gate there. His girl is about to go on in the competition for the gold medal, and she's suddenly so nervous she's squeaking. He grabs her by the shoulders and looks in her eyes and says, "You go out there like you're dancing the encore. You pretend you've already won the gold medal. When you look at the judges, you see people who are enjoying the final dance of a person they already awarded the gold medal. You look up at that blank scoreboard—it's full of 9.9's and 10.0's. It's over with. You're already the gold medalist."

And the young lady's got now stars in her eyes, and she's all pumped up and inspired and relaxed. And she goes out to skate with her whole being and mind believing that she's doing the encore of a gold medalist. She's totally relaxed, totally poised, and perfect, and the judges look at her and say, "She looks like a gold medalist already. Let's give it to her."

This is exactly what Vajradhara does in the world with a disciple. When you think of Vajradhara, please don't think of those funny pictures. Vajradhara is a holy beautiful being in jewels and the silk of the gods, and beaming with pure light. They come to a disciple, and they say, "You are on the edge. You have one more step to go. You have traveled for a million years. You are about to become

Vajradhara yourself. Now act like Vajradhara; think like Vajradhara; look like Vajradhara."

Be like that ice-skater. Believe you already won the gold medal. Then your every action will be the action of a pure enlightened angel. And the goodness of pretending to be Vajradhara will push you the last few feet into his or her paradise.

This is how Vajradhara teaches. Vajradhara only comes for people who are very, very close to the end. We're supposed to believe, and all the books agree, that our teacher is Vajradhara who came for the fourth time. This is now the fourth form. We're supposed to believe that we deserve to have Vajradhara, after two and a half thousand years and billions of people, come just for me.

You can think Jesus after two thousand years, showed himself to a few fortunate disciples after his death, and now has come again for one last time. Why? And how can you prove it? It doesn't seem like I would be worthy, of all the people who have lived and are living now. *[Crying.]* Why would Vajradhara or Jesus or Moses come, make a special trip just for me?

You don't get to find out until you eat refreshments. So please take a break—don't forget your hugs—and we'll start again when Winston rings the bell. [Break.]

To understand why Vajradhara might have come just for me, or Jesus, I think you need to take out your stone now and hold it in your hand. If someone's close to the platform, I think it would be nice if each retreatant had a stone.

Hold it, feel it, look at it. Hold it in your hands so you can't see it, and just feel it. I want to explain something about the emptiness of your stone. I hope you keep the stone, and maybe when you see it sometime you'll be reminded. Carry it in your purse or pocket—that's why we chose small ones. Try to remember.

The feel of the stone as you clasp your hand around it, the hardness of the stone, is a thing. That's one thing. And if you open your hand and look at the stone, the color and shape, which is what we call the stone, is a different thing.

What you see, which I will call the stone, and the hardness of the stone, are two different things. A blind man could feel the hardness of the stone, but not see "stone," so they are two different things. But obviously they are connected, and your mind

85

is connecting the hardness to the stone. The stone has a very basic energy, and that's hardness, the ability to stand up. If it didn't have hardness, it would just melt into a puddle. This energy in Buddhism is called the element of earth.

There are five energies, five great natural powers around us, very similar to the energies which modern physics explains. This stone has a predominance of the earth element, or solidity. These are not just old stupid ideas of a pre-scientific culture. These are profound insights into the energies which have created our world, by people in deep meditation. And they correspond to the same energies that were spoken about by Einstein or Oppenheimer.

The first of the five great elements or energies is called the element of space. It is place. The stone in your hand is occupying a place. If there was no energy called "place," it would simply collapse into itself and disappear. So the stone has the element of place, or space. It has an area in which to stand.

Try to understand what I say next. The connection between the stone and its hardness and the place where it is, is not a natural force or energy, because nothing is natural. There is no such thing as nature. This is a relationship between two or three things, which has been created by seeds in your own mind.

"Are you telling me that stones don't have to be hard? Are you telling me that under different circumstances, if I didn't have that seed in my mind this stone wouldn't be hard?" Yes, exactly.

"Are you proposing that there are places where stones don't even have space to be?" Yes.

"You're proposing that hardness is not part of the stone itself?" Right.

"So what?" *[Laughter.]*

Let's go through the other elements first. The traditional order is *namka, sa, chu, me, lung*. But the order for great meditators is the one I'm giving. First is place, or space. The second one is called "wind." What is the element of wind? It is motion itself, the moving of things. It is the motion of the blood in your veins, the motion of the breath coming in and out of your lungs, the motion of stars. We are travelling away from the greatest explosion in the history of our universe. We are not standing still. We are circling a sun, and both we and the sun are flying in another direction. Motion is needed for all life as we know it.

The third great element is water, and it means any kind of moisture. Even rocks have some water in them. Life, as we understand life, couldn't exist without water.

The fourth great element is fire, and it means warmth, warmth itself. The warmth of the sun, the warmth of your body, the sTrange spark of your body—where did it come from?

"So, I suppose you're suggesting that fire itself is a separate thing from its heat?" Yes.

"So you're saying that the fire of the very sun itself doesn't have to be hot if there's no mind to connect them?" Right.

The last element is earth, solidity, the so-called "natural" force, of solidity.

"So why are you talking about these things? It's cold; we don't have much time left."

There's something you have to understand about these great five energies. They're not natural. Fire is not hot by nature. Under different circumstances, fire would not be hot. If you didn't have a seed in your mind to experience fire as hot, you could put hand into fire undamaged. If you knew how to move the seeds of the great elements, with great prayer and meditation, you could remove the quality of liquidness from water, purposefully, and walk on it.

These are not just stories from the Bible or other places. These are great deep thinkers who have seen that even the greatest natural forces are perceived in objects because of our own minds. They can be changed.

"So what? What's it got to do with Vajradhara?"

Sometimes you wonder, "Why wasn't I born a little taller? How come I'm not so handsome? How come I can't get things like that other guy? How come I can't dance or play music like he or she?"

87

You worry about small things like that. But there are worlds where water doesn't work. There are worlds where nothing has warmth, because the beings who live there don't have enough goodness from their past behavior to see any warmth or water.

"What are you talking about? How could they live on a world with no water and no warmth? On a world where water doesn't even flow or stones aren't even hard? How could they live?" They don't; they die. They die in the moment of their birth in that place.

"How long can they stay there?" Their mind appears; their mind takes a form, and in that same moment, they die and disappear. For every person like you or me, there are billions like them.

"So what?" So time itself is an impression. Time itself is an image. Not everyone feels time the same way. In the moment of our time that it takes them to die without water or warmth, they experience thousands of years of pain. *(Geshe-la is sobbing.)* You're worried about how you look. They suffer. They don't ever experience anything else. You don't have to believe in some hell below the earth with a funny guy with a pitchfork. There are places where people have not had the goodness; they were not good enough to others to have water flow. There's no light. There's no warmth. They die in the instant they appear, and it takes thousands of our years. They feel it.

How many people like that, you can't even guess; it's beyond your thinking. Lord Buddha said. "If I told you, you would go mad in the moment that we speak." Because hardness is not a part of a stone. You see hardness because you were incalculably good. You have the honor to breathe and walk because of thousands upon thousands of holy thoughts and actions that you did before. And you worry about your hair. You are the ultimate evolution of millions and millions of lifetimes of effort by your past life.

It's not a coincidence that this earth is circling a source of warmth, and has water upon it and oxygen. It's not a coincidence that blood can flow through your veins. There are entire universes, billions of worlds, where nothing works right.

If the element of wind, if motion itself, is separated from the blood cells in you, we call it a heart attack. It's a miracle you're alive. Your body is made of millions of tiny parts—these are not a coincidence. Nobody made them; you did. Countless, countless, kind actions towards others, countless kind thoughts. Countless years of speaking kindly to others has pushed you into this world that you made. You're very lucky. It can't be said in words. You're beyond lucky. You are one in billions and billions and billions of suffering beings who die in the moment they are born. You are on the very edge of total perfection. You are about to become the holiest being there can be. I imagine a bullet about to hit a target. The front edge of the bullet is already touching the paper, but it hasn't gone through. You are that close.

The whole sky that you can see, the billions of stars, are places that work. They have warmth. They have the elements. But if you compare everything you can see to the places that don't work, it would be as if there were dark worlds under the ocean, and someone throws a rose petal on the ocean at night. Your whole universe, the galaxy that you can see at night, all the things that work, could fit inside the rose petal, and all the places where people are just born and die in the same moment are as big as the Pacific Ocean underneath you.

You are unspeakably special. Just to breathe air once, just to drink water once is unspeakably rare. But you are more than that. You live a life, you can speak, you can think, you can understand. You sense the truth of what I'm saying. You have been in those places. You have to try now to finish.

"How?" You need a teacher, Vajradhara.

So when you make your list of your teacher's good qualities and your teacher's flaws, which we did, and you get to the last one, it's a match made in heaven. When you leave this place and then wonder how it could be a match made in heaven—how can I meet the perfect being to help me?—try to remember the talk today. Vajradhara has come for you because you are unspeakably rare. You are a single diamond in the whole world.
"Oh, you must mean all of us here." No, I mean you.

"But there's lots of me's here." Each person has their own world. Each person has their own seeds. You are experiencing a different world from mine. You are the most precious and rare and impossible thing to happen in *your* world. Vajradhara has come for you. They don't send a boy to do a man's work.

In Tibet, there are six million people. When a Dalai Lama is born, they literally scour the country for the finest, most pure, wisest man, to be his teacher. The last one was Kyabje Trijang Rinpoche. This is your teacher's teacher. They don't let a fool teach the Dalai Lama, and you can see the results of his teacher's work in his living compassion. They wouldn't send anyone less than Vajradhara for you.

Verses:

The Magic of Empty Teachers

Day One: We need the perfect Teacher

Imagine the concert hall without one.
The blessing of living touch;
Instant depth, tricks and pitfalls,
Generations to the beginning.

A companion for life,
And like-minded friends;
Entry to a new world
Of people, places, and tools.

Someone to take you
Outside, beneath, and beyond yourself.
Don't be afraid to fish for the best;
Hook them with your service.

But first be clear
That what you want to learn
Is what They teach,
Or the marriage will never last.

In a world created
Moment to moment by imprints,
You master all things
By mastering one:

Serving others;
The high hard art of serving others.

Nothing for yourself;
Not even "I come to learn to serve,"
But rather "I come to serve and learn."
A relief to hear it said.

Learn to serve others
With a thousand hands,
From trifles
To deathlessness.

Day Two: What makes the perfect Teacher?

Find and become the perfect Teacher:
A Grandmaster with a big toolbox,
An open bag of candy,
A desert dandelion, and the air we breathe;

Stainless steel; a sculptor
Of every stone, with a master plan;
A mother bird
With a single motive.

Rocket fuel, and a match;
An echo, a taskmaster
Correcting and driving
With carrot and stick.

A gas pedal, a general
With the orders, a pillow,
An ant with winter coming,
Branching tunnels ready.

A chameleon on
The same old rock,
A lawn of grass,
An old temple gong.

Pruning shears
For a fresh sapling,
Mount Meru and
A rubber ball.

A teacher of learning and teaching;
And learning, teaching, an honor.
A builder glad to go to first grade
Even in their own school.

A proud poppa,

A push from the nest,
Genghis Khan and lieutenants,
A maker and passer of the torch.

A spider in a big web,
Peer revelry,
A free referral service;
A piggy bank, teddy bear, bureaucrat.

A golden magnet,
Symphony conductor,
An old pair of shoes
And an old hat.

An active player
By their own gameplan;
A kid single-pointed
On a double-scoop cone.

A gem carver,
A new edition of an old book,
Triple evolution,
Trail blazer and lion.

A golden retriever

And a koala bear,
Gold to file or cut or melt,
A scientist and detective.

A word to the wise,
A ballerina
One or two gathered
Or in the arena.

A seal
In a quiet sea,
A match
Made in heaven.

Day Three: What makes the Teacher perfect?

Both good and bad are imprints;
Nothing was ever anything else.
Learn to maintain the good ones
And learn to rip out the bad.

Pushed into this life
On the dying gasp
Of a great saint;
Living off another's credit.

Born on the down escalator
Turn and double-time up;
Very few get ahead,
Very few even notice.

"Look the other way."
"Compromise; make the best of it."
"Struggle with them."
"Move on."
"You are bad. Just stop it."
"Find some good in it."

"It's a test."

No, take control
Of your destiny:
Make your teacher perfect.

Locate and cut the imprint, new or old,
By doing the opposite for others, unilaterally.
A transformation will come, or did,
Or another or more, or both.

Hard or soft,
Use emptiness and
The act of truth;
We have no other choice.

In an empty teacher
There need be no will;
Not an excuse for the corrupt—
Their reward is the hell they hoped for.

And so the process
Of making your perfect Teacher
Makes you perfect;
This itself is the teaching
The magic of empty teachers.

Oh please do come
And use your teacher so.

Day Four: Why is the Teacher perfect?

"Vajradhara, Keeper of the Diamond,
Has come again."
But how can we be sure?
See and feel the stone.

There is space
And it is place
They live and die without it.

There is wind
And it is motion
They live and die without it

There is water
And it is moisture
They live and die without it

There is fire
And it is warmth
They live and die without it.

There is earth
And it stands up
They live and die without it.

Twilight worlds
Beneath a rose petal
On the open sea
In the dark of night

On the petal one diamond
So none less is sent;
No boy for the job,
No fool for a Dalai Lama.

He comes for the final step
And She is Vajradhara
For You are the coming Buddha,
You are the coming Buddha.

Acknowledgements

A big thank you to all the people who helped make the three-year retreat and these teachings happen.

To the retreatants Geshe Michael Roach, Lama Christie McNally, Lama Thubten Pelma, Lama Trisangma Watson, Lama Ora Maimes, and Ven Tenzin Chogkyi, thank you for inspiring us all and dedicating your lives to serve others.

It could not have happened without the caretakers. Thank you to Ven. Jigme Palmo (Elly van der Pas), Amber Moore and Ven Lobsang Chukyi (Anne Lindsey); Brian Pearson, Sarah Laitinen, Sid Johnson, Keith Nevin, Ven. Gyelse (Gail Deutsch), Mercedes Bahleda, and Deb Bye, who helped with everything.

And to Winston and Andrea McCullough, the directors of Diamond Mountain, and their wonderful children; Ted and Andrea Lemon, who shared their home; David and Susan Stumpf and everyone else who helped with construction; the 400 sponsors who helped pay the bills, and the 187 people who came to the teachings; our lamas and teachers Khen Rinpoche Geshe Lobsang Tharchin, Geshe Thubten Rinchen, Lama Zopa Rinpoche, Sir Gene Smith, Sharon Gannon, David Life, David Swenson, Lady Ruth Lauer, and Laura Donnelly; Jerry and Marjorie Dixon, who let us use their land; John Brady, John Stillwell, Salim Lee, and the many many secret angels, (you know who you are) who keep pretending that you are normal people.

The Quiet Retreat Teaching books were brought into the world by the work of many hands. Ven. Jigme Palmo of Diamond Mountain University Press morphed the teachings into book form. Special thanks for layout and cover design to Katey Fetchenhier. DMU-Press intern Michelle Ross was a huge help with printing logistics. Thank you for endless hours of proof-reading to Joel Crawford, Michela Wilson, Kelly Fetchenhier, Janice Sanders, Karlie Sanders, Cassie Heinle, Lindsay Nelson, and Michelle Ross. Big thank you to Marc Ross for spending his precious free hours making manuscript corrections. We would especially like to express boundless appreciation to Ven. Jigme Palmo for her uncanny ability to do 10 things at once—and do them all well.

And of course, our infinite gratitude to our Teacher, Geshe Michael Roach, without whom these extraordinary teachings would not exist.

www.ingramcontent.com/pod-product-compliance
Lightning Source LLC
Chambersburg PA
CBHW051818040426

42446CB00007B/724